The world of bad taste

Kitsch

The world of bad taste

Gillo Dorfles

with contributions by
John McHale, Karl Pawek, Ludwig Giesz, Lotte H. Eisner,
Ugo Volli, Vittorio Gregotti, Aleksa Celebonović
and essays by
Hermann Broch and Clement Greenberg

Studio Vista

Certain writers claim that the word derives from the English 'sketch', while others attribute it to the German verb *etwas verkitschen* ('knock off cheaply'). Giesz attributes it to *kitschen*, meaning *den Strassenschlamm zusammenscharren*, literally 'to collect rubbish from the street' 'which in effect is the interpretation closest to the concept of 'artistic rubbish' and might be linked to the term 'junk art'. This latter term has been used by English and American writers for a certain type of art which makes use of refuse taken bodily from the rubbish dump. The word *Kitschmensch*, meaning 'kitsch-man', is used by Giesz in his book and should I think be taken into the English language.

© 1968 Gabriele Mazzotta publishers, Milan
© This English translation 1969, Studio Vista Limited, London
First published in Great Britain in 1969
Reprinted 1970, 1973, 1975
by Studio Vista, 35 Red Lion Square, London WC1

Printed in the United States of America

Editorial assistance on the English-language edition by Vivienne Menkes
ISBN 0 289 70419 7

Contents

The terraced garden was liberally adorned with earthenware gnomes, mushrooms, and all kinds of lifelike animals; on a pedestal stood a mirrored glass sphere, which distorted faces most comically; there were also an aeolian harp, several grottoes, and a fountain whose streams made an ingenious figure in the air, while silver goldfish swam in its basin . . .
Over the outside door was an ingenious mechanism, activated by air pressure as the door closed, which played with a pleasing tinkle the opening bars of Strauss's *'Freut euch des Lebens'*.

THOMAS MANN
Confessions of Felix Krull, Confidence Man

Author's note

Although I have discussed the kitsch problem in various essays over a period of time, I have preferred, for the purpose of this volume, to insert essays by other authors which fit in with my own, so as to broaden a discussion which, I feel, a single author would not have been able to develop sufficiently.

So it seemed an opportune moment to reproduce two of the most important and interesting essays on kitsch, firstly one by Hermann Broch (written in 1933 and extended in 1950–1) which heralded the beginning of literature on the subject, and secondly one by Clement Greenberg, which was perhaps the first account of the relationship between kitsch and politics and was written in 1939.

Besides these I also commissioned a number of authors, all among the most highly qualified international authorities on the subject, to write the more specialized chapters, such as those on architecture (Gregotti), pornography (Volli), the 'plastic parthenon' (McHale), tourism (Giesz), cinema (L. H. Eisner), traditional kitsch (Čelebonović), etc.

Obviously it was not possible, even in such a thick volume, to review the whole panorama of kitsch: literary kitsch had to be left out because of the difficulty of giving sufficiently faithful kitsch (i.e. faithful in kitsch terms) translations in the various foreign-language editions of the book; and theatre and television kitsch had to be left out because they are to some extent part and parcel of cinema kitsch and kitsch in the figurative arts.

It is not customary to thank the publisher for publishing a book, but in this case an exception must be made. This work, born of constant collaboration between the writers and Gabriele Mazzotta, would never have been completed without his indefatigable search for visual material and for ideas which have helped to amplify the traditional concept of kitsch.

Kitsch is the daily art of our time, as the vase or the hymn was for earlier generations. For the sensibility it has that arbitrariness and importance which works take on when they are no longer noticeable elements of the environment.
There is no counterconcept to kitsch. Its antagonist is not an idea but reality. To do away with kitsch it is necessary to change the landscape, as it was necessary to change the landscape of Sardinia in order to get rid of the malerial mosquito.

Kitsch is art that follows established rules at a time when all rules in art are put into question by each artist.

HAROLD ROSENBERG
The Tradition of the New

INTRODUCTION
by Gillo Dorfles

Even if we can accept, with Hume, that 'beauty is not a quality inherent in things: it only exists in the mind of the beholder',[1] we cannot help being surprised at the fact that this 'seeing beauty' has changed so radically over the centuries, chiefly over the last two or three.

Obviously when we talk of remote antiquity, we base our arguments on mere suppositions and deductions; and when we talk of more recent antiquity, the Greeks or the Romans, we base our arguments on written documents, the accuracy of which is limited however, since they are difficult to interpret and are also concerned with what was then a very narrow social class. Yet I think I can fairly say that, in those days, and indeed in every age before our own, there

---

[1] David Hume; 'Of the Standard of Taste' in *Essays Moral, Political and Literary* (OUP, 1963 p. 234). 'Beauty is no quality in things themselves: it exists merely in the mind which contemplates them' and Hume goes on 'each mind perceives a different beauty. One person may even perceive deformity where another is sensible of beauty'. Obviously, in his enlightened scepticism, Hume did not take into account the fact that in ages other than our own (and his) 'absolute values' connected with the various characteristics of the period could have existed. As for the problem of taste in empirical aesthetics where the problem was not considered in any depth, the reader can refer to Lia Formigari: *The aesthetics of taste during the eighteenth century in England* (Sansoni, Florence 1962) and to Rossario Assunto; *Seasons and reasons in aesthetics* (Mursia, Milan, 1967). A bibliography of the literature on this basic problem of modern aesthetics would be almost impossible to compile. The most basic works can be found in the bibliography attached to this book.

was no such thing as 'really bad taste' i.e. kitsch.[2] I always felt that the reason for this was obvious and I referred to it in my *Oscillazioni del gusto (The Swings of Taste)*. In ages other than our own, particularly in antiquity, art had a completely different function compared to modern times; it was connected with religious, ethical or political subject matter, which made it in a way 'absolute', unchanging, eternal, (always of course within a given cultural milieu).

Today things are different; not because we see them in a different light but because the requirements of our civilization and of our society are different. This is why, when we talk about the art of the past, we will be able to – and we shall have to – apply a totally different judgement from the one we would apply today; and this is also why it would be absurd to refer to 'bad taste' in connection with the kind of art which was never concerned with the problem of taste. This means that the supposed bad taste which we sometimes think we can detect in ancient works of art (for the simple reason that they are not congenial, not 'in our blood', or not in fashion) is one thing; it is quite another to detect the *real* kitsch aspect in works of today or yesterday which not only clash with our own alleged good taste, but which represent a basically false interpretation of the aesthetic trends of their age – almost always for ethical, and therefore also political and technical reasons.

Further, the fact that today there is a prevailing tendency to refuse to apply the adjective 'beautiful' to the work of art – or rather to the 'artifact' – does not mean that one cannot easily differentiate between two artifacts on the basis of a 'pleasure scale' supplied by a certain number of experts.[3] This we feel is the only possible way to offer a value judgment and therefore a 'quality' judgment concerning a work of art (or even a purely technological piece) which meets certain demands of eurythmics, balance and finally, 'pleasantness'.

If there are no unbending laws to allow us to decide, once and for all, what the standard of taste is or is not, there are still these 'swings of taste' which I mentioned before, and we must surrender to the

---

[2] The word *kitsch* could derive etymologically from the English 'sketch' or, according to other opinions, from the German verb *'verkitschen'* ('to make cheap'). According to Giesz (Ludwig Giesz: *Phänomenologie des Kitsches* (Rothe, Heidelberg, 1960) which is without doubt the most complete work on the subject, the word *kitsch* could approximately be said to mean 'artistic rubbish'.

evidence of these facts which show us how taste does change according to the period and the historical situation, and so does the evaluation of a work of art.

There is also one fairly stable element – at least in our own day – on which we can rely; this can now be called kitsch unequivocally and is fated to remain as such, unless it is 'taken up' as an element of artistic sophistication and embodied in later work; but it will still be partial, temporary and paradoxical.

It is this element that I would like to examine in this book, trying to piece together in the various chapters all those factors and situations which are covered by the term kitsch. In this anthology of kitsch, my aim is to offer a kind of classified catalogue of the bad taste which prevails today, bearing in mind that it will be a history (or chronicle) which essentially 'coincides in time' and only partially 'through time'. This is because it is only if we take our own age, our own precise historical moment, as a starting point that we can try to catalogue such a delicate and vague subject which nevertheless scorches our hands, leaving permanent 'aesthetic scars'. Not only this, but because of those swings I mentioned, the reader will readily understand that he will have to see our choice as built up round a single point of view, a cultural pedestal as it were, a sociological attitude which is thoroughly subjective and personal. If anyone is not satisfied with our choice and finds some of the images artistic which we will present as pseudo-artistic, un-artistic, too bad! To us at least it will mean that our reader is really a 'kitsch-man' of the first water; and that the psychological test has worked properly. One more warning: our anthology includes, besides two essays written by Broch in 1933 and 1950–1 and another by Greenberg in 1939, a series of essays written specially for this volume by authors chosen from the best-qualified authorities on the subject in the various fields. The wide selection of illustrations shows mainly contemporary or recent examples, and for a special reason: contrary to what many people think, we should not talk about kitsch outside our own age; or at

---

[3] As for the possibility of a 'proairetic' assessment based on logical principles, the reader should refer to the volume by Georg Henrik von Wright *The Logic of Preference* (Edinburgh University Press, 1963) which contains the basis for a proairetic logic which would enable us to reach an evaluation of 'betterness' relying on an extremely rational and logical instrument.

least no earlier than the Baroque period. Before that period there were examples of mediocre art, works by lesser artists, by epigones and followers of great artists, works which were obviously not master-pieces; but which nevertheless were contained within the wider currents of fine art. Obviously there was even a hierarchy of artistic values, but there was no category which could be considered in a sense as art at the opposite end of the scale; something with the external characteristics of art, but which is in fact a falsification of art.

One must however be careful, as there is another misunderstanding of which we must not be guilty. All this does not mean suggesting again certain idealistic distinctions between 'poetry' and 'non-poetry' and stating that certain artistic products are not artistic because they have ethical, social, psychological and technical implications. On the contrary, I have more than once stated that poetry is art, but then so is industrial design; theatre can be art, as well as advertising, painting as well as graphic design and films.

That is why our anthology will provide few examples of kitsch in ancient times – even if to our modern eyes some works of art from the ancient world could look like kitsch; but how can we be sure that this is not the result of our own professional deformity?

One last point: one category which we will not show at all is that comprising modern artists' kitsch; although, to tell the truth, this category is thick with names and individual works. We are however, influenced by an innate generosity towards these representatives, however unworthy of modern art; to include them, with their names, in these pages would have meant either honouring them beyond their real worth or making them the object of public contempt. We have chosen to ignore them in the hope that they will improve in time or that posterity's judgment will change.

KITSCH

1 The archetypal image conjured up by the word 'kitsch' is the garden gnome, in this case represented by a series of Donald Ducks, Kennedy, Pope John, lions, pseudo-wells and (top right) the actual gnomes.

Kitsch *by Gillo Dorfles*

Most people these days are of the opinion that it is better not to discuss questions of taste, and that taste is no longer a separate entity which aesthetics must take into consideration. Recently, however, essays on taste have started to appear again,[1] not to mention all the books and essays written on the problem of taste in relation to the well-known distinction between the various artistic levels of low-brow, high-brow or, to follow McDonald's terminology, which has been so successful in the USA and elsewhere, the mid-cult, which indicates that kind of half-way culture, that mediocrity which is probably the most widespread of all and provides the artistic nourishment of the masses.[2]

[1]An important Italian essay on the problem is Galvano della Volpe's *La Critica del Gustu* (A Critique of Taste) (Feltrini, 1967, p. 63).

[2]The reader should refer above all to the well-known anthology by Bernard Rosenberg and David Manning White; *Mass Culture* (Free Press, 1957) cf. Dwight McDonald; *Against the American Grain* (Random House, New York, 1962) and particularly the chapter 'Masscult and Midcult'. On the problem of élite art and mass art, see also: Umberto Eco; *Apolcaliffide Integrati* (Apocaliptics and Integrated) (Bompiani, Milan, 1964) a chapter of which is devoted to the problems raised by kitsch, 'The structure of bad taste', taking into account literary kitsch and referring mainly to the works of Broch, Giesz and McDonald.

14

Even the word kitsch, once used only in Germany (probably because the problem was particularly acute there), has now spread and is used in the Anglo-Saxon countries as well as in Italy.

Further, whereas 'kitsch' was once applied mainly to works of art of a certain kind, in the last few years – particularly since the excellent essays on the subject written by Hermann Broch and Ludwig Giesz – the concept of the *Kitschmensch*[3] or kitsch-man has been extended to refer to the 'man of bad taste', i.e. the way in which a person of bad taste looks at, enjoys and acts when confronted with a work of art (either good or bad).

What proportion of modern mankind could be included in the ranks of kitsch-men? Almost certainly a very high percentage, though perhaps a smaller one than one would think. Very often the misunderstanding of modern art, of difficult, abstract, hermetic work (this covers much modern poetry, music or painting) is not due to an incompatibility between the public and art, but merely to a lack of preparation. It has often been proved (although we do not, and would not, need proof) that the average man, the man without prejudices, unaffected by the bug of 'mid-culture' and, above all, confronted by works of art continuously and patiently, will soon not only understand them, but also love them. There are endless instances of simple people – technicians, craftsmen, electrical workers, individuals involved in some of the new technological sciences – who have become fans of electronic music composers, kinetic artists and operators of programmed art just by meeting them; almost any modern artist could quote some such example. This would show how a great deal of the lack of understanding of modern art is undoubtedly due to lack of education and habit.

Quite different is the case of the kitsch-man[4] and of that sector of the public whose attitude towards works of art is definitely and hopelessly wrong. It is usually a matter of deliberate obtuseness which concerns modern art alone, or possibly 'difficult' art of the past i.e. the most serious type of work; it is a problem of individuals who believe that art should only produce pleasant, sugary feelings; or even that art should form a kind of 'condiment,' a kind of 'background

---

[3] The concept of kitsch-man, later adopted by Giesz, was defined by Herman Broch in the first place; *Einige Bemerkungen zum Problem des Kitsches* in *Dichten und Erkennen*, vol. 1 (Zurich, 1955, p. 295).

[4] This is what Giesz (pp. 28, 55 *op. cit.*) defines as the *Verkitschung von Kunstwerken* or 'kitschification' of masterpieces, which can take place, according to the author, because of a particular tendency to bad taste in the actual user.

music', a decoration, a status symbol even, as a way of shining in one's social circle; in no case should it be a serious matter, a tiring exercise, an involved and critical activity . . .

That is why this kind of public will demonstrate its lack of understanding or faulty interpretation of the work of art not only when they stand in front of modern art, but also when they are confronted with the great works of antiquity which they think they understand. Such people will judge Raphael as if he were a painter of picture postcards; Wagner or Verdi on the basis of the romantic content of their *libretti* rather than of the quality of their music; Antonello da Messina or Morandi on the 'pretty' or 'decorative' aspect of their paintings, rather than on the truly pictorial aspect. They will find the most involved and improbable historical novels interesting because of their romantic element.

If this aspect, which concerns the use of art rather than its creation, is reasonably typical of our age, I believe that there is one more aspect which is equally restricted to our own day, since it never existed before: I refer to the presence around us of a number of pieces, both works of art and objects which merely belong to the customs and fashion of a certain age, which are affected by curious, unpredictable and ever-changing factors with regard to a 'taste' assessment. We all know how fervently creative the period called Art Nouveau[5] was in the fields of interior decoration, ceramics, glass and architecture, and we also know how the majority of such work, only a few decades afterwards, was completely abandoned and despised, only to be brought back to sudden fame and exaltation over the past ten years.

What happened with the Art Nouveau style happened again in connection with what is known as the furniture of our grand-parents, or even of our great-grandparents, and it happens over and over again, with annual variations, to the fashionability of the various styles in the various countries and periods (we witnessed at one stage the establishment of the 'Empire' style, followed by Louis XVI, which gave way to Baroque and even to the seventeenth century).

How are we to take this phenomenon? This should not be difficult to answer in the case of a more or less pronounced fashion for certain styles which have by now become classical, i.e. catalogued, registered and recognized as 'artistic': the phenomenon in this case is mainly due to the state of the market, or to advertising, or to some affinity

[5] On the revaluation of Art Nouveau see the chapter 'The example of Liberty' in my book *Swings of taste (Oscillazioni del Gusto)* and also Friedrich Ahlers-Hestermann; *Stilwende* (Berlin, 1941) Dolf Sterberger; *Jugendstil* (Hamburg, 1956), and Stephan Tschudi Madsen; *Sources of Art Nouveau* (Oslo, 1956, London, 1967).

between different styles (the fashion for Far-Eastern art at the beginning of the century (plate 2), the emergence of the various revivals during the nineteenth century (plates 3 and 4), English Gothic (plates 5 and 6), American colonial, etc.).

2 This 'oriental boudoir' forms the sitting room in a London flat in Gloucester Square, which appeared in the first volume (no. 6) of the *Studio* in 1893.

It is more difficult to answer in the case of objects and works which are 'assumed' to be artistic merely to satisfy a certain temporary need, only to be rejected, forgotten or even despised quite soon when the mood changes. Obviously, in this case, fashion prevails over art; and we will often see the emergence of examples of the most authentic type of kitsch (we only need to think of those ultra-modern kitchens covered in colonial trappings which have replaced the modern, functional, clinically white kitchens of a few years ago).

One more example – again very common – occurs each time a single element or a whole work of art is 'transferred' from its real status and used for a different purpose from the one for which it was created. This is what happened when the great monuments of the past were used for purposes other than the original ones; the alabaster copies of the Leaning Tower of Pisa, for instance, are not kitsch

17

3–6 Examples of the revival which took place in the nineteenth century. The leap in space (from the Middle-East) and in time (from the Gothic style) represented an extremely refined motif to the architect Cordier, who designed buildings in 1850.

precisely because they are copied in a different material but also because they have exploited a 'visible deviation from the rule' (the angle of the tower) and made it a source of curiosity and attraction. They have therefore degraded the whole of the wonderful 'Miracle Square' to the level of kitsch imitation. (We should also note that the very word 'curiosity' which has just come to my lips, or rather to my pen, is always steeped in kitsch; what else are those 'curios' much sought-after by American tourists during their package tours abroad but the purest kitsch?)

The same has happened to so many of Liszt's and Chopin's tunes (two composers far from minor, far from easy if studied in their own context) which have been dragged down to the level of sentimental songs; not to mention the use of other masterpieces, Michelangelo's *Moses,* Leonardo's *Mona Lisa* (plates 10 and 11), the *Sistine Madonna* by Raphael, Cellini's *Perseus* (plate 12), which have become symbols

of kitsch by being vulgarly reproduced and known not for their real value but for a sentimental or technical substitute of these values.

We could even venture to say that what happens to kitsch is somewhat parallel – only in reverse – to what happens when one element in a song is taken out of context so as to increase the power of its artistic message; poetry, music and painting often make use of this trick, which consists of extracting a work of art, or part of it, from its usual context and inserting it somewhere else, thus achieving the alienation of the message and increasing its powers of information.

In the case of kitsch, we have something along these lines, but in the opposite direction: *The Last Supper* by Leonardo is extracted from its usual environment (the Hall of the Graces) and translated into a stained glass window, which is in its turn inserted into a marble chapel at the Forest Lawn Memorial, and cast in white plaster (plate 13) – we can easily imagine with what result. The same happens whenever a great work of art (like Leonardo's *Mona Lisa*) is used, say, in a cheese advertisement, for a poster or for a beauty contest (plates 7, 8, 9).

Another remarkable thing, connected with kitsch and referred to by McHale[6], is the frequency with which exact copies of masterpieces (ancient or modern), mass-produced in good-quality materials such

[6] Cf. the essay by John McHale in this book.

7–8 The Mona Lisa is an inexhaustible source of kitsch. The marvellous smile is here reproduced on the package for a brand of cheese and as an advertisement for a man-made fibre.

19

as marble or bronze, can be obtained and marketed. If mass-production is suitable for industrial goods and several modern works of art which were specially designed for the production line, this is certainly not true in the case of works from the past, which were conceived as unique, and were intended to remain unique. To display a fake *Apollo Belvedere* or a false *Nike of Samothrace* (plates 14 and 15) or Cellini's *Perseus* can only increase the kitsch atmosphere of the place rather than improve on it.

9 'The painters, members of the jury for the Mona Lisa Grand Prix, have awarded the title *Mona Lisa 1958* to a model whose grace, beauty and refinement embody the aesthetic of today's ideal woman. She is Luce Bona, who has been chosen as the symbol of the celebrated Mona Lisa. Luce Bona, poses for the photographer in a frame for the Mona Lisa Grand Prix' (Agency hand-out 28-2-1958).

10 The Mona Lisa myth appears once more against the tiles of a shower.

11 A spectacles-case

◀ 12 Cellini's *Perseus*, 1ft 6in high, reproduced in yellow plaster.

13 *The Last Supper* converted into 3D for the bedside table.

21

14 Via the pages of an American catalogue, you can order 'authentic masterpieces' by post in white or black, at low prices.

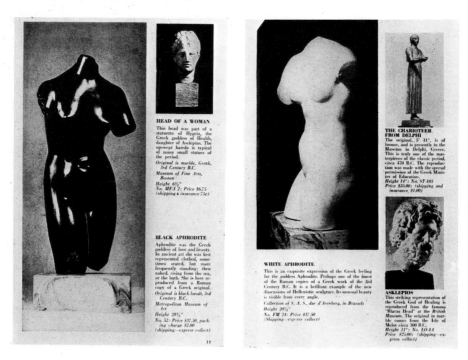

On the contrary – and this is the other side of the coin – some of the most ghastly objects can be transformed into artistically positive elements, if not masterpieces, if used in a certain way, in environments which aim to create a sophisticated atmosphere through the devaluation/revaluation of those objects, not to mention the fantastic transformation which can be undergone by a single element (apparently or even authentically kitsch) when it belongs to a whole, a totality which is aesthetically acceptable and effective. One gigantic example: the stupendous silhouette of New York in its entirety can-

15 'Classical garden statues' and 'architectural structures' in the yard of a factory which specializes in such items.

not help but be considered as aesthetically admirable for its authentic architectural qualities as well as for its grandeur; but let us analyze it in detail: most likely many of the skyscrapers (particularly those built in the Babylonian style, but also the steel ones in Curtain Wall) and the statues (such as the one in Rockefeller Center, plate 19), not to mention the Cloisters (plate 16-18) could definitely be considered kitsch. Yet who would dream of mentioning bad taste when confronted with a scene which is artistic when viewed as a whole?

23

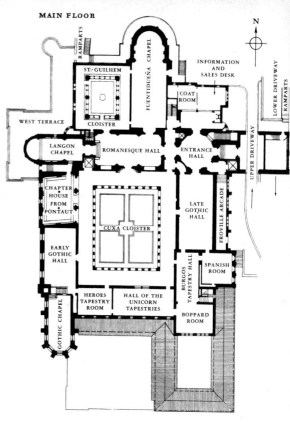

16–18 The monumental complex of The Cloisters, inaugurated in 1938 in Fort Tryon Park, owes its existence to the generosity of John D. Rockefeller Jr. The structure is entirely modern but incorporates authentic architectural features from the cloisters of medieval monasteries. Authentic objects and works of art are displayed in the halls, which are always full of tourists.

MAIN FLOOR

RAMPARTS

ST.-GUILHEM

FUENTIDUEÑA CHAPEL

INFORMATION AND SALES DESK

COAT ROOM

WEST TERRACE

CLOISTER

LANGON CHAPEL

ROMANESQUE HALL

ENTRANCE HALL

LOWER DRIVEWAY

RAMPARTS

UPPER DRIVEWAY

CHAPTER HOUSE FROM PONTAUT

CUXA CLOISTER

LATE GOTHIC HALL

FROVILLE ARCADE

EARLY GOTHIC HALL

BURGOS TAPESTRY HALL

SPANISH ROOM

HEROES TAPESTRY ROOM

HALL OF THE UNICORN TAPESTRIES

GOTHIC CHAPEL

BOPPARD ROOM

19 *right* The Rockefeller Center ▶

In a similar way one could consider the Wright cushions in Taliesin West to be bad taste, instead of admiring the splendid 'internal space' of the building which houses them. This is why we will never be altogether sure that fake marble columns, papier-mâché statues, wood imitation wallpapers, glass animals from Murano and even mother-of-pearl shells and Brazilian hardstone in the shape of ashtrays, although themselves undoubtedly kitsch, are beyond recovery. They will be saved if they are de-mythified and used in a different context and atmosphere. The trouble starts when we re-mythify – or rather idolize – the demythified objects and look upon them as expressions of the highest degree of sophistication: we then produce 'hyper-kitsch', 'kitsch squared', the kitsch of the detractors of middle-class kitsch, the creators of the super-snob kitsch. Kitsch belongs to all the arts, to all man's forms of expression. In this book I will not deal with literary kitsch (which is an inexhaustible source of amazing material) for an obvious reason: this kind of kitsch is almost always untranslatable and does not survive the transformation which language is constantly subject to, even within a brief lapse of time; it is almost impossible to judge the 'kitschiness' of a translated passage or even of a piece written some twenty years before. At first sight even one of Leopardi's poems, not to mention Manzoni's *Odes*, sounds kitsch today (unless we place them in their right historical context by means of hard philological work). Expressions, sentences, individual words which are no longer used or are even in definitely bad taste to-day would have been perfectly acceptable some ten years ago. Besides, it is extremely difficult to lay down general rules for literary kitsch which could be applied to all languages (apart from the too obviously kitsch paragraphs taken from the romanticized tales written for Victorian girls or from the reports on the social life of royalty which still pester our magazines). Therefore, since our aim is to present a collective panorama of international kitsch, it would not be enough to limit ourselves to examples from our own language and it would almost certainly be ineffective to produce translated examples from other languages.

I will not therefore consider literary kitsch, but will hint, even if only vaguely, at musical kitsch, which is as international as visual kitsch; unfortunately, however, we will not be able to produce examples of this kind of kitsch.

Here again, in the case of music – especially 'New Music' – the problem of kitsch is particularly urgent: nothing could be further away from a piece of 'consumer music',[7] enjoyed and adored by the

[7] The problem of 'consumer music' has been a knotty one for recent writers. The reader should refer to the book by Straniero and others, *Le canzoni della cattiva coscienza: La musica leggera in Italia* (Bompiani, 1964), with an introduction by Umberto Eco.

26

masses, than a piece of the new modern music, enjoyed and enjoyable to only a few initiated individuals. It looks as if, in this field, we have a fixed rule as a basis for our discussion. And yet we are far from reaching an agreement, even though the problem was the subject of the most recent discussions and lectures during the latest (1967) 'Tagung' at the Darmstadt Institute of New Music.[8]

One of the main theories which came up at Darmstadt was formulated by Lars-Ulrich Abraham, who tried to base his opinions on 'taste' as a category of musical teaching. He was, however, opposed by the majority of the speakers, as very few people are willing to consider 'taste' as a category. One should not forget, however, that the concept of taste, which, as everyone knows, can be referred back to the English and Scottish empiricists of the seventeenth and eighteenth centuries – Hume, Gerard, Burke etc. – has been extremely important, particularly from the sociological point of view, and it cannot therefore be disposed of too easily.

Some people believe that in a modern environment the very concept of taste no longer performs any function at all, given the modern 'pluralistic' kind of musical culture which is therefore divided into various classes. It is obvious that all distinctions between cultured music and consumer music are impossible if based on a consideration of intervals, rhythm and the use of certain musical techniques.

The problem of kitsch music cannot be resolved so easily[9]; it is not enough to state that taste is not a category applicable to music. Nor can the value of a musical piece be determined on the basis of its popularity, since this depends on the use of certain musical paramaters which will make of a pentatonical melody a tune which is difficult for a European but not for a Japanese.

Even if we limit our research to our own age and to western civilization, there is no doubt that the gap between cultured music and consumer music is such as to give the impression that the two groups belong to quite different worlds or universes. And yet I believe that even within these over-large categories, it is still possible to talk about kitsch. Kitsch music does and will exist even when aimed at a musical élite (and many will be the creators of authentic and original modern compositions who will have made their work more acceptable by inserting slightly emotional elements, which can somehow rouse

---

[8] The *Tagung* mentioned here opened with a lecture by Rudolf Stephan; *'Von der Notwendigkeit über Musik zu Sprechen.'*

[9] Kitsch music according to Carl Dalhaus, who was one of the speakers in Darmstadt, should be traced back to the coming together of sentimentality and composition technique. For an accurate account of the work carried out at Darmstadt, the article by Reinhardt Oehlschlagel: *Geschmack, Trivialitat, Kritik,* in *Frankfurter Zeitung,* 25-4-1967, should be read.

20 Beethoven's 'Eroica' in a pictorial interpretation

21 *Frau Musika*, a *fin-de-siècle* illustration which clearly shows not only the attitude of the kitsch-man, but even a dog enraptured by the melody.

the public's sentimentality, or which – while adopting dodecatonic or punctual formulas – will produce some pleasurable tune which is easily borrowed from a completely different kind of music).

It is a fact, however, that the field in which music will be a greater help – a greater comfort – in our search for kitsch elements is in the attitude of the user rather than that of the composer. The kitsch-man (plates 20 and 21) is most clearly visible in his way of listening to music; the kitsch-man who can turn even the great Johann Sebastian into kitsch, by attaching to his rigorous and even pedantic compositions some sentimental intentions which he never even dreamt of having; or mistaking the religious impulse of a great deal of sacred music for easy 'sentimentality', suitable for a completely different occasion. This is the central and most important factor in the identification of kitsch, not only musical kitsch but also literary, cinematographic and even 'naturalistic' kitsch: the attitude of the individual when confronted with artistic and natural phenomena, which are observed from that particular point of view which immediately transforms them into something inferior, false, sentimental and no longer genuine.

But when we discuss kitsch and consider it as limited mainly to our age, I feel it is necessary to take into account the importance which the advent of the machine had in determining it, both in producing and reproducing works of art as a unique means of communication and expression.

It is far from difficult to recognize a certain synchronism between the appearance of certain kitsch factors and that of mechanical and subsequently electric and electronic methods in the reproduction and transmission of art.

This does not mean to say that there is an absolute connection between the two processes, as we shall see; but I wish to underline the fact that only the easy (if not inferior) reproduction and the quick distribution of art (or pseudo-art) objects has made it possible for one of the factors we are interested in to come to the surface. This is the problem of cultural industrialization; the fact, that is, that even culture – both in its creation and in its consumption – is affected by some of the methods which now influence the whole, or almost the whole of our production and organizational system; this problem is of ever-increasing importance. On the one hand, because it would be foolish not to take advantage – or to be unable to – of the powerful and often effective means which the most up-to-date forms of technology are offering us, even for cultural purposes; on the other, because it would be just as dangerous not to be aware of the dangers, misunderstandings and traps which confront us whenever the two sectors of culture and industry meet or even just barely touch.

Obviously, research into the problems of the industrialization of culture and the mass-media which the world has learnt to use has increased considerably over the last few years. There are detractors of such media as well as fans; we have heard jubilant voices extolling the victory of mass-media over traditional media and panic-stricken voices complaining about their emergence and excessive intrusion.

It would be enough to mention the book by Marshall McLuhan *Understanding Media* which over the past three or four years was so successful in the USA and elsewhere; or the well-known anthologies devoted to the problems of mass-media and mass-art, such as the one by Rosenberg and White.

But the kind of cultural industrialization which I wish to deal with briefly, since it is one of the main causes of the rise of kitsch, is the kind which appeals to the imagination, or, if one can use these terms, to the fantastic and creative activity of man; that activity which usually was, or should have been, a strictly personal possession of individuals and which on the contrary – through the use of some of the mass-media – has become as public an activity as all the others.

The visions, the dreams, the indistinct and vague ocean of our imaginary activity are enslaved by new mechanical methods of transmission and communication the moment they become their prey. There is, of course, a positive aspect as well as a negative one (not just the negative aspect as many people like to believe). The intervention of the machine can, I believe, be considered beneficial whenever it alleviates the exploitation of man by his neighbour; nor do I think it right to throw all the blame on the greater amount of spare time which man enjoys nowadays (or should enjoy) as if this were the cause of the greater aridity of his creative imagination and of his progressive tendency towards an exclusively hedonistic use of his spare time. Even if this does in fact happen, the machine or industry are not necessarily to blame. Unfortunately, mass-culture, being as it is at the root of the new distribution of time, has killed all ability to distinguish between art and life; all trace of a 'rite' in the handing out of cultural and aesthetic nourishment by the mass media (radio, TV, magazines, cinema) has been lost, and this lack of the ritual element has brought about an indifference in the onlooker when he is faced with the different kinds of transmissions and manifestations which are forced upon him.

It is therefore advisable to analyze this factor carefully, more for its anthropological aspect and influence than for its strictly aesthetic aspect. One of the mistakes made by people who have carried out research in this field is to have assumed aesthetic implications before solving the sociological and psychological problems which underlay it. Foremost among them is the experimental factor, which plays an important part in our use of the new mass-media.

Another relevant aspect is the lack of an authentic 'lived experience' obtained through the new media: a phenomenon that anyone can observe by himself and on himself. The sight of reproduced images – via photography, cinema, television and magazines – is no longer capable of transmitting a truly 'lived' experience, although it does allow us to store up ideas promptly and rapidly, as has been amply proved. The result is a split between the eventual acquisition of the idea and the real and actual *Erlebnis* of the images we see. What happens is more or less what we experience when we visit a foreign country and then see it reproduced in a cinema. The halo of images and sounds, tastes, smells and atmospheres offered by the foreign country, which will remain unmistakeable in our memory, is reduced to a pale image, a dream ghost, when transmitted through the new mechanical means of communication.

I have dealt in the past with the problem of falsification of the image produced by modern methods of reproduction, and I feel that this problem is not only closely connected with the problem of taste and bad taste but is also under-estimated by both the public and the critics. There is no doubt that the large-scale reproduction of works of art – both visual and musical, ancient and modern – by means of the new technical methods represents one of the most surprising and noticeable characteristics of the recent cultural evolution. But if we have to recognize the mass-production of industrial objects originally intended for such treatment as perfectly authentic, we must regard all reproductions of unique works which were conceived as unrepeatable as the equivalent of real forgeries.

Even if faithful reproduction has made it possible to spread artistic and historical knowledge to wide sections of the population, we should not forget that these days the mania for reproduction has resulted in the paradox of works and objects which are only apparently and extrinsically similar to the original being treasured. We only have to think of the innumerable copies of the Sistine Madonna, of the Parthenons, Belvedere Apollos and Leaning Towers of Pisa; their artistic value has promptly become an exclusively kitsch value because they are reproductions, or, even more, because of the way these ex-masterpieces are used, enjoyed and idolized by kitsch-men, who buy them and fill their homes with them. Very often reproductions of these works – both ancient and modern, a typical example being coloured reproductions of the Impressionists, Van Gogh and Gauguin – have lost all respect for faithfulness to scale and nuances of colour, for the overall feeling of the image; this means that they not only offer the public facsimiles which are out-and-out approximations, but also, and this is even more surprising, make the public feel that they are more attractive, more beautiful and more effective than the originals.

Another aspect of this general attitude is represented by the many copies of antique (or modern) masterpieces obtainable at low cost through the direct mail catalogues. These copies only apparently encourage culture and taste: what they really do is to incite the public to put the authentic masterpiece on the same level as the mediocre or even obscene copy. The industrialization of culture, spreading to the world of artistic images, has brought with it a heightening of the traditional distinctions between the various socio-cultural strata. Mass-culture has acquired completely different characteristics (or so it seems) from the typical features of élite culture and has contributed to the spreading and triumph of kitsch art.

If however this pseudo-culture has no form of differentiation in enjoyment (i.e. as I said above there is no longer a *privileged moment* in administering artistic nourishment, and, contrary to what happened in the past, all traces of ritual have been lost, thus depriving the work of art of that aura of mystery and sacredness which once characterized it), we cannot deny that even this levelling type of culture needs some kind of differentiation if it is to be accepted by the general public. This explains the incessant quest for new products, which have never been issued before and are in some way individualized. And this gives rise to yet more examples of kitsch. One of the most obvious and powerful examples of this demand for novelty for its own sake, without any aesthetic or technical motivation, which causes the frequent emergence of kitsch objects, consists of the well-known process known as styling. This kind of styling, or 'face-lift', is applied to industrial design products exclusively for marketing reasons, on the part of the buyer, or to encourage a thirst for acquiring an effective status symbol via such products.

Among the most typical features in these new artistic *'genres'* (born of films, condensed versions, industrial design, consumer music etc. and often coinciding with the advent of kitsch) we can observe the following: the collectivization and sub-division of the work of art, and hence the inevitable subjection of the individual work to team-work and consequently to a collective standardization which introduces into mass-produced art some of the elements belonging to a higher level of culture; and vice versa.

At times, some of the products initially conceived and created for a cultured élite become merely a reason for fashion, expensive and

22–23 Modigliani *above* and Morandi *below*
transferred onto ceramics and mosaic respectively.

snobbish, appealing to that 'upper class' (exclusively from the economic point of view) which is equated culturally with the worst type of midcult.

This factor is not often enough dealt with by sociologists examining the problem of mass art: i.e. the fact that the economic-cum-financial-cum-social élite is not the same as the cultural élite, and the incompetence and reaction which characterizes the financial upper class with respect to avant-garde art (i.e. genuine avant-garde art) and their acceptance of such art merely because, or when, it has become fashionable and therefore sought-after and expensive. It so happens that the élite culture tends to resist the integration and standardization which is typical of mass and consumer products: but unfortunately this resistance is often based mainly on an element of idolization, which only comes to light later, when the products of a false avant-garde will have proved empty and obsolete. For this reason the products of the pseudo avant-garde often have, when compared with the real ones, no more than the appearance of illegibility, obscurity and a facile, deliberately shocking *épater les bourgeois* element.

Another aspect, typically fetishistic this time, is the way certain genuine types of avant-garde art borrow elements from highly trivial consumer products. We have seen various examples of this in much recent pop art (Jasper Johns, Rauschenberg) where the element borrowed from the consumer products (Coca Cola bottles, photographs, toothpaste, tins) becomes aesthetically valid because of the very fact that it is included in the painting in such a way as to create an object the uniqueness of which is difficult to communicate (unless it is converted into some 'noble' material, as in the case of certain fruit cast in bronze by Cavaliere). One wonders whether this habit of translating trivial products taken from standardized and de-individualized production into the realm of élite art should be regarded as positive, or whether it means that the avant-garde artist himself sometimes prefers the kind of art which he appears officially to despise.

The idolization and snobbish cult of avant-garde art can be included within the boundaries of kitsch. It is undoubtedly difficult to distinguish; but we only need to pick up a so-called avant-garde magazine from any of the industrialized countries, to be immediately aware of its existence. We will notice for instance examples of nauseating and naïve imitations of Joyce, Beckett, or Kafka, where literature is concerned; of Duchamp, Schwitters, the great pop artists in the field of painting; or of Stockhausen and Cage in that of music. What does the kitsch element consist of here? It lies in the fact that the people who made these camouflages of authentic avant-garde art have isolated one single aspect of the artistic phenomenon they try to imitate and which originally had a genuine creative value, raising it to the level of a pattern but thus depriving it of any novelty value and therefore of any informative impulse. They have for example made use of the well-known and much abused process of combining various linguistic elements as if they were preparing some sort of quiz for an illustrated weekly. The moment of perplexity followed by discovery which was valid in Joyce or Duchamp is thus translated into a mere search of the 'where is the mistake?' variety typical of certain puzzle pictures. They have borrowed certain commonplaces from the great authors: the habit of including polyglot words in provincial texts (often ignoring the real meaning of foreign words of which they do not know the correct pronunciation, which is often the basis of the pun). All this is equivalent – only on a different level – to what we have seen in the case of the novelette, the Western and the consumer song.

The element of falseness appears everywhere in such cases of hyper-kitsch: love, grief, birth and death are transformed into super-ficial emotions or hedonistic witticisms. Thus the hard work accomplished for their own consumption by a Joyce, a Proust, a Klee or a Mondrian becomes work accomplished with the sole aim of being published or exhibited; merely to demonstrate one's up-to-dateness; and merely to confuse the out-of-date critic or reporter.

This is an extreme case, often overlooked, of what could be called cultural élite kitsch: the bad taste of the high culture. The existence of products which belong to high culture only in their external appearance, their make-up, their slang, but which are in fact part of the very same kitsch, that cultural substitute revealed in the crime novel or the romantic novel, in juke-box music, in the mass-appeal film. I would like to close this chapter with this kind of hyper-kitsch, since it is a good way of demonstrating how the danger of artistic falsification can be hidden anywhere, without sparing any stratum of society. It is not the prerogative of the lower classes nor of the economically higher classes (even if it does often prefer the middle and upper middle classes) and finally does not spare even those people who like to think of themselves as the possessors of the most elevated type of avant-garde culture.

24–25 Orpheus's song is the inspiration behind a ceramic fountain for a *de-luxe* hall; Giuseppe Verdi's head becomes a book-end and a spinning wheel-cum-lamp is displayed in the background among the oriental and *fin-de-siècle* statuettes.

26 Reproduction Gaugins and Rousseaus add an artistic note to the bathroom and transfigure its purely functional aspect.

MYTH AND KITSCH
by Gillo Dorfles

The field which nowadays is probably more susceptible than others to the influence of kitsch and which demonstrates both the aesthetic importance and the existential importance of this deviation, is that of the myth.

Among those who have studied the modern myth and the emergence of mythopoetic and mythogogic factors in our civilization are Mircea Eliade, Lévi-Strauss, Ricoeur, Roland Barthes and Gilbert Durand. It is important to note how the particular mythicizing tendency which gave rise to some of the greatest works of art, religion and literature produced by man in the ancient world is still present, although it no longer gives rise to imposing epics, powerful legends and religious tales, but to squalid fetishistic phenomena of inferior publicity.

I dealt with this facet of the problem in my book *Nuovi Riti, Nuovi Miti* (New rites, new myths) (Turin, 1965) where I tried to draw a distinction between an authentic and positive *mythopoetic* energy and a spurious *mythagogic* projection which is almost always deplorable and ill-omened insofar as it is compulsory and heterodirected and gives rise to the fetishization and mystification of its own achievements. What could be more symptomatic of kitsch than certain typical modern myths, such as the fascist and Nazi myths, the myth of the sportsman, the champion, the pop singer, the film star, all of whom become heroes adored by the crowd, even if only for a brief season?

The process by which the man in the street, harassed by radio, TV and the other mass media, attributes to a certain personality (almost always cunningly and forcibly manipulated by a propagandist and commercial network) those virtues which will raise him to the level of a mythical hero cannot but be related to the category with which we are concerned here, since it demonstrates its main characteristics: those qualities of substitution, falsification, sentimentality, coarseness and vulgarity in the 'image' (which is to be understood here in the sense of the corporate image as used by advertizing to create the specific and symbolic connotation for a firm or product).

The case of Rita Pavone or Celentano in Italy, the Beatles and the Rolling Stones in England, Johnny Halliday and Sylvie Vartan in France, are all good examples.

It is dangerous in this instance to refer to specific names since one of the characteristics of the modern pseudo-myth is its rapid and inevitable obsolescence, whereby a figure who is famous becomes absolutely unknown in a matter of two to five years. Anyone who has watched a show by Rita Pavone or the Beatles (huge theatres packed

27 The Beatles' Rolls-Royce

28 The Beatles' period of meditation in the 'spartan cottages' of the Maharishi Mahesh Yogi's Academy has certainly served the purpose of increasing their mythical aura.

with crowds of fans, girls screaming hysterically as if they were in the presence of some divinity, ready to sacrifice themselves to it like the vestals of some new religious mystery) will certainly have noticed the cunning way in which these stars calculate the effect of the most typical details of their clothing and apparatus. It is precisely the existence of this 'magic uniform' which has allowed such stupid and utterly dull figures as Superman and Batman to survive: a bat-shaped cape, a body-stocking with a gigantic S (all in the purest kitsch style of course) are enough to raise these garments to the level of sacred attributes, as if they were precious amulets or relics endowed with miraculous properties.

The taste is distinctive.
The man is Sean Connery.
The Bourbon is JIM BEAM.

SEE SEAN CONNERY IN "YOU ONLY LIVE TWICE."

29 The figure of James Bond lends itself to this advertisement for a Bourbon which is reputed to be Sean Connery's personal taste.

There is perhaps a precise reason why – as in the case of the Beatles – a deliberate effort was made to recover this sacredness, when these likeable young men spent a holiday with a well-known (but how authentic we do not know) Indian holy man on the banks of the Gan-

30 The idiotic figures of Batman and Robin raised to the level of unsophisticated decorative fetishes.

ges. The mere fact that they tried to extract a sacred initiation from the very sources of the legend, so that they could combine it with the mythical overtone they already possessed, confirms my assertions: the false myth attempts to link up with a real myth so as to become more effective and results in an appearance or attitude which is indisputably kitsch.

It would, of course, be easy to object that not all these mass idols are absolutely inferior, that some of the songs written or sung by the Beatles or the Rolling Stones should not be underestimated, that certain attitudes, even if basically geared to publicity, do still contribute to a particular atmosphere which will eventually lead to a certain taste in clothing, fashion, colour, and so on.

I do not intend to underestimate the importance of customs and fashion in determining the particular outline of a cultural era but what I do wish to point out is the obvious lack of proportion between the data on which the mythagogic element is based, and their socio-aesthetic outcome. Can we place Orpheus and the Beatles on the same level? Moses and Hitler? paladins and sports champions?

We might perhaps think of Nazism and the French Revolution, the feats of the cosmonauts and those of Christopher Columbus as equally important and decisive from the historical point of view; but what still seems indisputable in spite of everything is the fact that the authentic myth of the past did not show any trace of the kitsch element which is so often found today.

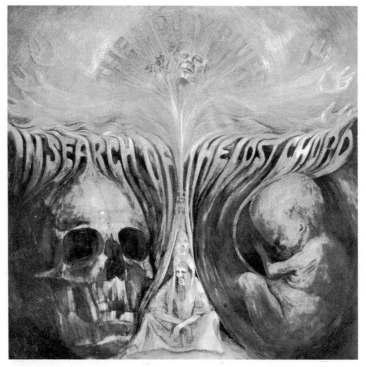

31 In this cover of a beat record some of the elements of Buddhist mysticism are debased to typically kitsch material.

A great deal of the ritual apparatus, figurative paraphernalia, decorations and emblems which accompanied any movement such as the fascist or Nazi movements (this is more true of the former than of the latter, perhaps because it was less genuine) was decidedly kitsch: the imperial eagles, the kepis with their tassels, the salute and the goose-step (as we shall see more clearly when dealing with politi-

42

cal kitsch) all had a definite note of poor taste; the same poor taste which we can detect once more in manifestations of false rituals such as the Ku Klux Klan, the Masonic lodges and certain pseudo-religions (particularly in the USA) such as that of the Mormons, Christian Science and the countless Protestant sects, where both the ritual and the scenic apparatus are not based on any authentic religious tradi-

32 A New York shop window. Alongside monstrous masks and typically kitsch souvenirs hangs the threatening face of Fidel Castro.

tion and for that reason can easily degenerate into kitsch ... A phenomenon that cannot go unobserved is the vast number of ritual elements which take advantage, even in our own day, of many of the ceremonies which accompany displays based on supposedly occult values or of the political and religious significance they have for society, once these have been institutionalized. I am thinking of the flags, emblems and badges of the various more or less exclusive clubs, particularly when they are based on a real or assumed tradition; and even the paraphernalia of the various yacht clubs, golf clubs, equestrian societies, hunting clubs, etc., in which one can seldom detect traces of up-to-date taste, or of elements borrowed from modern and avant-garde art and dress. It is almost as if any club – whether religious or lay, political or gymnastic – felt it necessary to employ the aspects of the worst type or of a soured and dusty taste. And what about the cups, medals or uniforms of the various mystic and theosophic sects?

33 Sado-masochism for the masses in this American chamber of horrors.

34 There is a strong kitsch element in
this advertisement for a book with an
attractive title.

I have often felt moved to remark on the curious and almost sacri-
legious degradation of venerable and undoubtedly authentic occult
symbols as soon as they become the prey of the mythagogic tendency
and false rituality which we have been discussing. The cross, the
swastika, the triangle with the divine eye, the star of David, the signs
of the zodiac etc., the whole of that sacred alphabet which in the past
derived (as it still could) transcendental values from glorious mysteries, immediately becomes false when coupled with pseudo-mythi-
cal institutions; it becomes obsolete, unfashionable, unsuitable. This
is probably why one so often notices what I should like to call witches'
kitsch, fortune-tellers' kitsch, astrologers' kitsch. It seems to me that
this phenomenon has not yet been properly analyzed and that it

45

deserves closer examination. I have often noticed when visiting fortune-tellers (many of whom, however, are in fact endowed with extra-sensory gifts) that all the properties they use and even their attitude are undoubtedly linked to old-fashioned Victorian customs and are surrounded by a definite kitsch atmosphere. What is even stranger is the fact that we can definitely regard as kitsch a large amount of the paraphernalia and the individuals who use them. Even the ectoplasms so fully illustrated in certain classics on spiritualism and meta-physics are often veiled in this type of poor and old-fashioned taste. So how do we interpret this phenomenon? Are the spirits of the dead behind the times or tied up with some obsolete fashion? Obviously I do not want to get involved in such delicate matters; nor do I want to speak with disrespect of phenomena which are difficult to judge. It would seem to me that the only answer is to realize that what I have said does not apply to those circles and people who are seriously and scientifically interested in such problems, but rather those individuals who, although endowed with instinctive extra-sensory gifts, exploit them for profit rather than in the interests of research; in so doing they use all the gadgets which, whether they wish it or not, can only lapse into clichés full of bad taste and ambiguity. Once again, therefore, the presence of kitsch whenever mystical elements and depraved rituals are in evidence clearly demonstrates how important (in this case, not only from the aesthetic point of view but also from the ethical and sociological angle) it is that the presence of the type of phenomena I have tried to outline should be noted.

Summing up this brief sortie into the sector of myths and rites, we could conclude that mythopoetic trends often prevail today. These trends can be beneficial: they can lead to the birth of new myths which can in turn give rise to works of art or social and political achievements. Often, on the other hand, the mythagogic aspect is the prevailing one, with its tendency to attribute mythical and ritual values to elements, situations and people which are not suited to them, can hardly bear them and should not be invested with them. In this case, it almost always happens that the myth becomes kitsch, a kitsch-myth is born, and it is all the more to be deplored because it tends to penetrate further, thanks to the energy and magic intensity which are characteristic of the genuine myth and which the pseudo-myth can reproduce, even if only temporarily.

35 The 'miraculous hands' of that modern myth, Dr Barnard, in a colour insert in ▶
a women's magazine.

CHRIS
BARNARD

le mani miracolose

The mere fact of being able to talk of a kitsch-myth (as well as of a kitsch element in religion, in patriotism, in the family and in death, as we shall see in later chapters) proves once more that kitsch exploits irrational, fantastic and even sub- or pre-conscious elements.

The revaluation of the mythical element in the study of symbolism (as carried out by Ernst Cassirer along the lines which lead from Vico to Schelling and to the new mythologists of our own days: Kereny, Durand, la Langer etc.) has proved the fundamental significance which should still be attributed to the irrational aspect of our thoughts and our faculties for learning. It is therefore easy to understand that it is this irrational aspect, rather than the rational one, which should exploit kitsch to trap the unwary.

If a mytho-symbolic component is always present in every kind of art, it does not necessarily follow that each work of art should be regarded as mystified or mystifying, as some people tend to believe; it is more realistic to admit that in the kind of pseudo-art which we call kitsch, the mythifying aspect appears more obviously and more frequently.

the anti-hero HOSTILITY Dart Board

● Draw a bead on your frustrations . . . fancied, frenzied, real . . . just for fun! Our 14" dart boards capture the photographic images of some of your favorite anti-heroes . . . plus 3 imported darts to help you aim straight and to the point.

$3.98

● Choose LBJ, Lady Bird, Humphrey, Castro, Hochi Minn, De Gaulle, Nasser, Nixon, Bobby Kennedy, Reagan or Sigmund Freud.
● CUSTOM HOSTILITY BOARDS: Throw darts at your boss, your mother-in-law, your psychiatrist, etc. Send us a photo or negative which we'll return with a 10½" dart board game of your personal photo choice.................$10.00
● HIS 'N HERS DART GAMES: No couple should be without one! He's on one side, she's on the other, or you might want one of the kiddies.
$15.00
Anti-hero Hostility boards available for immed. del.; allow 3 weeks for Custom and His 'N Her Boards. (Be sure to send a black and white photo or negative); add 45c postage per dart game ordered.

36 An 'anti-myth dart board'. Aim darts at whoever you fancy, from de Gaulle to Ho Chi Minh to the portrait of your psychoanalyst.

NOTES ON THE PROBLEM OF KITSCH
by Hermann Broch

With your permission I shall begin with a warning: do not expect any rigid and neat definitions. Philosophizing is always a game of prestige played with the clouds, and aesthetic philosophy follows this rule just as much. So if I say now and again that that cloud up there looks like a camel, please be as polite as Polonius was and bear with me. Otherwise I am afraid that at the end of this lecture you will find that too many questions have been left open, to which I could only reply in a study of kitsch in three volumes (which I would rather not write anyway).

In addition, I shall not talk strictly about art, but about a fixed form of behaviour with regard to life. Kitsch could not, in fact, either emerge or prosper without the existence of kitsch-man, the lover of kitsch; as a producer of art he produces kitsch and as a consumer of art is prepared to acquire it and pay quite handsomely for it. In a broad sense art always reflects the image of contemporary man, and if kitsch represents falsehood (it is often so defined, and rightly so), this falsehood falls back on the person in need of it, on the person who uses this highly considerate mirror so as to be able to recognize himself in the counterfeit image it throws back of him and to confess his own lies (with a delight which is to a certain extent sincere). This is the phenomenon with which we shall concern ourselves.

When dealing with phenomena which have to do with the history of the mind it is always necessary to reconstruct the environment in which they arose and on which they have an influence; first of all architecture, which represents a fairly characteristic expression of each historical period; when we think of the Asian civilizations, of Egypt, of the Gothic period, the Renaissance and the Baroque, architectonic images of these civilizations and historical periods are the first things which spring to mind. But what architectonic image comes to mind when we think of the Romanticism of the nineteenth century?

None. Of course much of European Romanticism was contained within a framework of facades in the neo-classical-Biedermeier style (and American Romanticism in the colonial style); but only because the buildings of the previous generation were still standing. Romanticism itself did not in fact produce a single architect capable of raising his style to the level of any of the styles of neo-classicism: the Berlin *Schinkel* style for example. Its first architectonic expression was horrible: whitewashed or bare-brick Gothic with battlemented trimmings, which held the field from the 1820s to the 1840s and was used for stations and public buildings as well as for private villas and working-class districts; after this this type of kitsch (for it really was kitsch) had to give way to the even more violent neo-Renaissance and neo-Baroque styles. Not to mention the fact that the extremely rapid industrialization and development of large cities did not give architecture enough time to adjust itself to its new tasks, and it was therefore forced to embark on a desperate and groping search. No, *Schinkel* had, for example, provided solutions for shops and public buildings which were perfectly adequate for their functional requirements, and which were indeed quite modern. Why then, instead of welcoming these proposals, were stations and lower-class dwellings built in Gothick kitsch? The answer is simple. Because kitsch, not *Schinkel*, corresponded to the spirit of the times and because the functionalism of *Schinkel* did not seem beautiful enough when taste was orientated towards kitsch. What interested people was beauty, the fine effect, decoration.

Great Romantic art was totally inadequate in this setting, thanks to this kitsch which was not yet the ambiance of Beethoven, Schubert, Byron, Shelley, Keats and Novalis, but already that of Stendhal, Delacroix, Turner, Berlioz, Chopin, Eichendorff, Tieck and Brentano. How can one combine this authenticity and high degree of genuine and brilliant expressive force (and so much inner expression in the case of German lyricism) with so much decorative emphasis? And why has this decorative cult become so insipid, and therefore kitsch, while the milder decorativeness of the Baroque (every age has its passion for decoration) offered an adequate framework even for someone like Bach, not to mention Handel and Mozart, who tended to like effect? Architectural kitsch certainly constitutes a completely adequate framework for a considerable part of the artistic production

37 A spectacular setting for the film on Berlioz, *Symphonie Fantastique* (1942), is not enough to dispel the painful elements in the film.

of the time. Walter Scott, for example, revealed an undeniable and quite fatal affinity with the neo-Gothic style of the time, and one cannot imagine an environment better suited to Paul de Kock, Balzac's esteemed contemporary. The environment, therefore, appears inadequate only for the greatest works of genius and there was an abundance of such work at this time); it is quite adequate for everything which did not attain an absolute level of value, such as the musical dramas of Weber (although they do nonetheless deserve respect). A clear line of demarcation seems to run straight across the artistic production of the age, dividing it into two basic and radically different groups, without any intermediary gradations: on the one hand we have work which reveals cosmic aspirations, and, on the other, kitsch. Which group is representative of the age? Was it hall-marked by kitsch (which would tend to make us consider the great Romantic work of art as something surpassing it), or should one say conversely that Romanticism was responsible for kitsch?

Many things, chiefly the lack of average values, testify in favour of a prevalence of kitsch. The stylistic tone of an age is generally determined solely by the work of genius, but it draws its substance from the average work. The history of art is full of such minor works. Paintings by the Gothic and Renaissance schools belong to this category; the same could be said, without exception, of the compositions of all the many organists of the seventeenth and eighteenth centuries, who, even if they were not all Bachs, accomplished extremely valuable work. Also in the architectonic field, the last of the master-builders, before the advent of Romanticism was absolute master of his trade. Romanticism, on the other hand, was incapable of producing average values. Every slip from the lofty level of genius was immediately transformed into a disastrous fall from the cosmic heights to kitsch. Take Berlioz, for example, whose decorative and consciously effective style (a very French feature) is only just bearable: not only does Berlioz use associations which are sensational and foreign to music, but he even quite shamelessly sets his *Faust* to the rhythm of a spiritedly orchestrated Racoczy march. Even intro-verted German Romanticism always moves along a razor's edge, continually running the risk of falling into kitsch; this can happen even in a fine piece of poetry, not through deliberate irony (as in Heine) but more simply because of the poet's inability to maintain the cosmic tension. To many of you it may seem blasphemous for me to use Germany's best-loved Romantic poet to illustrate my argument, but I have done so in order to show how swift and headlong the fall can be. Let us look at Eichendorff's *Abendlandschaft* (Evening Land-scape). The first six lines:

> *Der Hirt bläst seine Weise,*
> *Von fern ein Schuss noch fällt,*
> *Die Wälder rauschen leise*
> *Und Ströme tief im Feld.*
> *Nur hinter jenem Hügel*
> *Noch spielt der Abendschein*[1]

[1] The shepherd plays his tune,/a last shot dies far off,/the woods rustle softly/and streams flow deep in the fields./The last glow of evening/still plays behind that lone hill.

are certainly among the most beautiful German lyric poetry ever written in their calm descriptive precision. These perfect lines are then followed by a couplet which is no more than an insipid and sentimental imitation of popular poetry:

Oh hätt ich, hätt ich Flügel,
Zu fliegen da hinein![2]

Only in a very few of his poems, *Reisesehnsucht* for example, or the *Greisenlied,* does Eichendorff succeed in sustaining the cosmic tension from beginning to end; the others seem to be fated to be shipwrecked on the reef of sentimentality contained in the last lines and to drift ashore towards the beaches of kitsch. This justifies what I have said about the lack of average values in Romanticism, and the reader himself, once he has managed to leave behind his youthful impressions, will find further proof of this in Chamisso's *Frauenliebe* or *Mateo Falcone.* Conversely, kitsch definitely does contain average values. Kitsch can be good, bad or even original, and while I am going to blaspheme once again by saying that Wagner is one of the highest peaks never touched by kitsch, I would not hesitate to add that even Tchaikovsky failed to escape it.

It seems, then, that there is every justification for considering the nineteenth century as the century of kitsch instead of the century of Romanticism? But if this verdict is fair, why is it so? The Marxist would say that the bourgeoisie degardes art with imitation goods, which is why the full flowering of industrial capitalism could not help but provoke the flowering of kitsch as well (the fact that the Marxist living in Russia today is confronted by a powerful and posthumous second crop tends to be overlooked by him because of his love of theory). But it is better to set aside what is happening in Russia and to concentrate on the facts in the West; if we anticipate the outcome of this study, we can say that however deep the mark left by kitsch on the nineteenth century, it in fact derives predominantly from the spiritual attitude we define as Romanticism.

The middle class emerged in the nineteenth century as a class destined to win power in the fairly near future. Driven by its urge for power, it had, on the one hand, to assimilate the traditional patrimony of the courtly-feudal class, changing it as it went along, and, on the other, to reaffirm its own original tradition, which was a revolutionary tempo.

[2]Oh had I wings, had I wings/to soar there yonder!

53

The courtly tradition was predominantly an aesthetic one: its ethical conception was confined to set mystical portrayals of a God-willed hierarchy, to which, quite independently of any enlightened rational scepticism, men had to adjust with an attitude which was at once amused and stoical; in return, they were entitled to make their lives a work of art and to procure for themselves, by means of unbridled debauchery of the senses and of the mind, all the pleasures possible, including those of art. In other words – and this is the privilege of any ruling class – they had the right to embellish their lives with exuberant decorative splendour, which would be all the more exuberant because it was subject to the formal influence of Baroque. The bourgeois tradition, on the other hand, had a fundamentally ethical stamp. In Protestant countries this was influenced exclusively by the ascetic Puritan-Calvinist ideal, while in Catholic countries the parallel revolutionary movement (which was also a protest against the *libertinage* of the *ancien régime*) had made *virtue* into a universal guiding principle. In both Catholic and Protestant countries man was thus spurred on to put his great spirit of sacrifice to the test – sometimes for love of the State, sometimes for love of God. In both cases alike, this ethical imperative was founded exclusively on reason, and in both cases this was opposed to art and decoration, or at least indifferent to them. The middle classes had to remain absolutely faithful to their severe tradition, so as to be able to make the distinction between themselves and the feudal aristocracy, seeing themselves as the class destined to come to power in its stead. Why then, did they ever have to submit to the law of assimilation and appropriate the aristocratic tradition, which was still moving in a direction diametrically opposed to their own? Were they driven to do so by their passion for art? Or merely by a spirit of imitation? Or, more simply still, had their ascetic spirit run out in the meantime? All these factors must have played their part, as they then found themselves in the midst of the Enlightenment, and, as we know, the Enlightenment did not favour the ascetic spirit (it is not mere chance that it produced *libertinage*). On the other hand the spirit of enlightenment was not to be quenched in the age of industrialization, nor was it possible to restore the old faith which had provided the incentive for asceticism. To preserve this ascetic spirit, despite this, but without abandoning the rationalism of *libertinage* was, therefore, the insoluble question that the bourgeoisie had to solve.

The problem would probably have remained unsolved if the bourgeoisie had not still carried within them, ever since their most distant origins (as far back as the Renaissance), those tendencies which were

54

38 An 1896 illustration: dry-point for the magazine *Pan* titled *The Pair of Centaurs* by Max Pietschmann.

in turn destined to produce Romanticism: the tendencies of reform. The Reformation came about due to a great discovery, which was partly mystical and partly theological and rational: this was the discovery of the awareness of the absolute, the infinite, of the divine conscience of the human mind. This brought the act of revelation into every single human mind and thereby saddled it with the responsibility of faith, a responsibility which the Church had previously borne. The mind settled the account and became presumptuous and boastful.

It became presumptuous because it had been assigned this cosmic and divine task, and it became boastful because it was well aware that it had been given too much credit, that it had been loaded with a responsibility which exceeded its resources. This is the origin of Romanticism; here is the origin of, on the one hand, the exaltation of the man who is full of spiritual (and artistic) energy and who tries to elevate the wretched daily round of life on earth to an absolute or pseudo-absolute sphere, and, on the other, the terror of the man who senses the risk involved. That uncertainty which is peculiar to the Romantic mind and which is timorous and hesitant, longing to turn back and hide in the bosom of the Church, to take refuge once again in its absolute certainty, derives in fact from this mixture of exaltation and terror. To forestall this relapse, the Calvinist-Puritan movement pointed out the exclusive guarantee of the Holy Scriptures and forced men to accept that cold asceticism, totally foreign to any form of effusion, which was destined to become the middle-class way of life. But when asceticism began to lose its strict dominance, the bourgeois felt that the veto on exaltation had also been swept away, so he exalted, paradoxically, to save the ascetic tradition. Any asceticism, any repression of pleasure has its sexual centre of gravity. Puritanism certainly did not impose a monastic type of chastity, but strict monogamy. It was precisely this monogamy that was to be reaffirmed and reinforced; all the more so because in this way it could strike at the heart of *libertinage*. Monogamous love was saved by being intensified to a level of exaltation which at one time had been severely condemned by asceticism. Puritan frigidity was transposed into passion. Every casual act of love in everyday life was raised to the astral plane; the level of the absolute (or rather of the pseudo-absolute) was transformed into an incorruptible and eternal Tristan-and-Isolde-style love. In so doing it simply introduced the most terrestrial aspects of life into the eternal and immortal kingdom – the worldly aspect *par excellence* –, which explains that atmosphere of quite indecent necrophilia which so largely dominates Romantic literature. Listen to what Novalis says about this type of fidelity beyond death in his *Lied der Toten* (Song of the Dead):

Leiser Wünsche süsses Plaudern
Hören wir allein und schauen
Immerdar in sel'ge Augen,
Schmecken nichts als Mund und Kuss.
Alles, was wir nur berühren,
Wird zu heissen Balsamfrüchten,
Wird zu weichen zarten Brüsten,
Opfer kühuer Lust.
Immer wächst und blüht Verlangen,
Am Geliebten festzuhangen,
Ihn im Innern zu empfangen,
Eins mit ihm zu sein.
Seinem Durste nicht zu wehren,
Sich im Wechsel zu verzehren,
Von einander sich zu nähren,
Von einander nur allein.
So in Lieb' und hoher Vollust
Sind wir immerdar versunken,
Seit der wilde trübe Funken
Jener Welt erlosch.[3]

39 *Libertinage* carried to the pseudo-absolute sphere of the sublimation of love in this picture from *Salon*.

[3] All we hear is soft desires,/sweet murmuring, and look/eternally into beloved eyes,/taste only mouth and kisses./Everything at our mere touch/becomes the hot fruit of balsam,/soft and tender breasts,/sacrificed to fierce longing./Desire grows and blossoms ceaselessly,/desire to cling to the beloved,/take the beloved within us,/be at one with him,/to nourish and be nourished /by ourselves alone./Thus are we plunged forever/in love and sublime desire,/until the wild and troubled spark/of this world is out.

Here fidelity is literally raised to a position of power. The new age – i.e, the age of the middle classes – wants monogamy, but at the same time wants to enjoy all the pleasures of *libertinage,* in an even more concentrated form if possible. They are thus not content to raise the monogamous sexual act to the stars; the stars, and everything else that is eternal, are obliged to come down to earth to concern themselves with men's sexual lives and enable them to reach the highest pitch of pleasure. The means of obtaining this lies with the imagination over-kindled by exaltation. *Werther* is the first work in which this type of exaltation appears; and in fact the spirit of an age is always made manifest for the first time by a genius (no wonder then that Napoleon felt *Werther* to be so close to his own spirit that he carried it everywhere with him, although his life was not in the least like Werther's). It was Novalis, however, who took the consequences of Wertherian exaltation to extremes: which resulted in high Romanticism. And it seems almost natural that unbridled Romantic exaltation also brought with it a revival of Catholic tendencies.

But having falsely overcome the ascetic tradition, or rather having opted for this new false celebration of asceticism, the middle classes then tended to find in it not only solutions to their own erotic and sexual problems, but also a compromise between their own Puritan and ascetic conception of art and their own love of decoration. Even if courtly-feudal decorative art secretly appealed to them, they had to disdain it so as to remain faithful to their own ascetic tradition; and if they were now able to grant freedom to their own taste for decoration, the result was to be a form of art that was more serious, more elevated and more cosmic than that of their predecessors. One is immediately struck by the parallel with the erotic and sentimental situation (man does not have a very rich range of variations in his attitudes and actions): the aesthetic pleasures of the libertine are looked down on, but the bourgeois would also like to indulge in them, even if on a higher plane. And in fact just as, in the sphere of erotic relationships, love itself has to come down from its celestial heights to consecrate and take part in every human act of love, so in the aesthetic field beauty has to be incarnated in every work of art and consecrate it. Eichendorff has expressed this attitude in a not very poetic sonnet, *Der Dichter* (the Poet):

Das Leben hat zum Ritter ihn geschlagen
Er soll der Schönheit neid'sche Kerker lichten;
Dass nicht sich alle götterlos vernichten,
Soll er die Götter zu beschworen wagen.[4]

Almost all the ingredients proposed for the artist by the poet's age and generation are contained in this recipe (which Eichendorff fortunately did not follow in his own poetry). He should not only represent the aristocracy of mankind, he should not only be the 'knight', the 'prince of poetry', but also the sublime priest whose duty it is to ensure the survival of the gods by practising his creed, i.e. by his artistic production; as a priest he must be in contact with the gods to induce them to restore beauty to the world and to make her descend from her celestial heights to the level of mortal things in every work of art. Schiller, who expressed himself rather more lucidly on this point, seems to have been forgotten. This conception is none other than a forewarning of a sort of religion of beauty which is not very different from the religion of reason which the French Revolution tried to establish when, having dethroned God, it saw the need of basing its *virtue* on something absolute, and accordingly had to invent its 'Goddess of Reason'. But as things proceed rationally in the kingdom of reason, this 'Goddess of Reason' was soon forgotten. In the kingdom of art, on the other hand, absurdities are much less disturbing, so that the horrible spectre of divine beauty that enters or is introduced into the work of art continues to lurk in literature throughout the nineteenth century, and indeed passes on into the twentieth century as well without any break in continuity. This divine beauty is the fundamental symbol of all the symbolist schools and is at the root of their aspiration to set up a new religion of beauty (which one can detect both in the Pre-Raphaelites and in Mallarmé or George). Without damaging the greatness of Mallarmé or the important artistic work of George, or even the admittedly considerably lesser value of the Pre-Raphaelites, we can safely say that the goddess of beauty in art is the goddess kitsch.

One can raise the objection that art always generates beauty. This is true, just as it is true that every cognitive act generates truth. But has there ever been a human eye capable of contemplating 'the' beauty or 'the' truth? The answer is certainly no, because both – and I do not need to quote Schiller here – are mere Platonic objectives,

[4]Life has marked him as a knight;/his job to light the envious prisons holding beauty captive;/ to stop everything becoming profane/he must dare to invoke the gods.

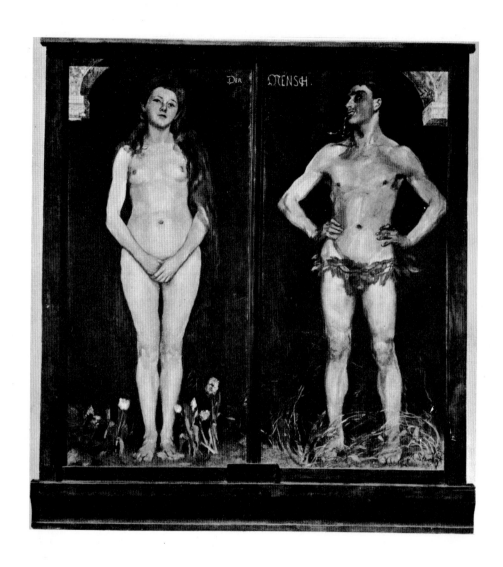

40 Beauty and primordial sexuality in a late eighteenth-century German painting. (Max Slevogt – *The Couple*).

adjectives that have become nouns. For earth-bound man beauty and truth are only accessible in the form of single beautiful or true phenomena. A scientist who puts no more than his own love of truth into his research does not get very far; he needs, rather, an absolute dedication to the object of his research, he needs logic and intuition; and if luck (which plays a rather more important part than the idea of truth in such cases) is in his favour, truth will appear all by itself when his work or his experiments come to an end. The same is true of the artist. He, too, has to subject himself unconditionally to the object; his capacity to listen to the secret voice of the object (independently of the fact that it presents itself as an exterior or interior object), to seek out the laws that it obeys – think of Dürer's experiments with perspective, or Rembrandt's experiments with light – does not depend on the artist's love of beauty. His truth, like the scientists', is, on the contrary, a ripe fruit that he will pluck from the successful work. And yet why are the scientist and the artist driven onwards incessantly by the whip of obsession for the object? What causes this love of exploration? Is it perhaps the *terra incognita* of what exists that fascinates him? No: the truly unknown cannot seduce him; he is seduced only by what is just beginning to be sensed: the man who can foresee a new shred of reality must manage to formulate it, so as to be able to make it exist. In science and art alike the important thing is the creation of new expressions of reality, and if this process is interrupted not only would there be no more art or science, but man himself would also disappear, since he differs from animals precisely because of his capacity to discover and create something new. The artist who limits himself merely to a search for new areas of beauty creates sensations, not art. Art is made up of intuitions about reality, and is superior to kitsch solely thanks to these intuitions. If this were not so one could certainly content oneself with previously discovered spheres of beauty, e.g. with Egyptian sculpture, which is without doubt unsurpassable.

We have reached the point where we can illustrate why kitsch resulted from Romanticism, and why it must be considered a *specific* product of Romanticism. And in fact if knowledge, and in particular scientific knowledge, can be defined as an infinitely developing logical system, the same can be said of art in its totality: in the first case, the *telos* of the system (a goal suspended in infinity and at an infinite distance) is truth; in the second it is beauty. In both cases the final objective is the Platonic idea. It seems regrettable that love is also a Platonic idea, an idea that cannot be attained by means of the many unions to which man is constrained (this, incidentally, explains why love songs are all so sad); but as love can scarcely be considered as a system, there may be some hope left for it. But where-ever the goal is unquestionably unattainable, i.e. in structures which, in the manner of science and art, move relentlessly forward according to some inner logic from one discovery to the next, which means that the goal remains outside the system, then the system may and should be called open. Romanticism is inclined in exactly the opposite direction. It wishes to make the Platonic idea of art – beauty – the immediate and tangible goal for any work of art. In this way it at least partly removes the systematic aspect of art. Yet, insofar as art remains a system, the system becomes closed; the infinite system becomes a finite system. Academic art, which involves a continual search for rules of beauty, with which all works of art must comply, makes things finite in a similar manner. We cannot, of course, identify Romanticism with academic art, nor are kitsch and academic art identical (although the latter is one of the most fruitful areas for the influence of kitsch); but nor should we overlook the common denominator underlying all these phenomena, which consists of their tendency to render the system finite. And as this process constitutes the basic precondition of every form of kitsch, but at the same time owes its existence to the specific structure of Romanticism (i.e. to the process by which the mundane is raised to the level of the eternal), we can say that Romanticism, without therefore being kitsch itself, is the mother of kitsch and that there are moments when the child becomes so like its mother that one cannot differentiate between them.

I know I have become rather too abstract; and I also know that to make an abstraction concrete one has to follow it up with a second abstraction and then a third. Kitsch is certainly not 'bad art'; it forms its own closed system, which is lodged like a foreign body in the over-all system of art, or which, if you prefer, appears alongside it. Its relationship to art can be compared – and this is more than a mere metaphor – to the relationship between the system of the Anti-Christ and the system of Christ. Every system of values, if attacked from the outside in its autonomy, can become distorted and corrupt: a form of Christianity that forces priests to bless cannons and tanks is as close to kitsch as any literature that exalts the well-loved ruling house or the well-loved leader, or the well-loved field-marshal or the well-loved president. The enemy within, however, is more dangerous than these attacks from outside: every system is dialectically capable of developing its own anti-system and is indeed compelled to do so. The danger is all the greater when at first glance the system and the anti-system appear to be identical and it is hard to see that the former is open and

62

the latter closed. The Anti-Christ looks like Christ, acts and speaks like Christ, but is all the same Lucifer. What then is the sign that enables one to see this difference? An open system, like the Christian one, is an ethical system: it provides man with the necessary directions for him to act as a man. The hints given by a closed system, on the other hand, (even if they are covered with a veneer of ethics) are no more than simple rules of play; i.e. it transforms that part of human life which is in its control into a game that can no longer be valued as ethical, but only as aesthetic. This conceptual cycle is anything but simple – as I warned you earlier – but it can become clearer if you remember that a player is ethically well-behaved if he is thoroughly versed in the rules of the game and acts in accordance with them. He is not concerned with anything else going on round him with the result that, when he has to play his part, he will calmly let a man drown at his side. This man is the prisoner of a purely conventional system of symbols, and even if these symbols are copied from some sort of reality, the system is still a system of imitation. We have already mentioned the grotesque religions of beauty and reason. At this stage we can also add political religions. Here again it is a question of imitation, of religions of imitation, which therefore carry within them the seeds of evil. Kitsch is also a system of imitation. It can resemble the system of art in every detail, above all when it is handled by masters such as Wagner, the French dramatists (Sardou, for example) or – to take an example from painting – someone like Dali, but the element of imitation is still bound to show through. The kitsch system requires its followers to 'work beautifully', while the art system issues the ethical order: 'Work well'. Kitsch is the element of evil in the value system of art.

Of course, an ethical system cannot do without conventions and since this is so, the man who sticks to it is inevitably constrained, at least to a certain degree, to aestheticize his tasks and to transform them into works of art which correspond to convention. In accordance with the exclusively aesthetic character of the convention which he follows, the libertine will make his life a sybaritic work of art, while the monk, who lives according to an ethical convention, will allow himself to be conceived as a transcendental work of art. Both are unequivocal, and conform to reality, the sybarite's life being suited to worldly reality; the monk's to celestial reality.

Can the same be said of a life inspired by kitsch? The original convention which underlies it is exaltation, or rather hypocritical exaltation, since it tries to unite heaven and earth in an absolutely false relationship. Into what type of work of art, or rather artifice,

41 Salvador Dali 'improvizes' his usual living picture in his luxurious summer residence.

does kitsch try to transform human life? The answer is simple: into a neurotic work of art, i.e. one which imposes a completely unreal convention on reality, thus imprisoning it in a false schema. High-Romanticism scattered so many tragedies of love and individual or dual suicides throughout the world precisely because the neurotic, wandering about among unreal conventions which have assumed for him the value of symbols, does not notice that he is continually confusing aesthetic and ethical categories, and is obeying false commandments. The only category that emerges from this confusion is that of kitsch and its evil quality, which is what caused all those suicides. It is the wickedness of an existence based on universal hypocrisy, astray in an immense tangle of sentiments and conventions. It is superfluous to stress that the middle classes deceived themselves by saying that they had won a complete victory; throughout the nineteenth century they pretended that they had inaugurated great art and defeated *libertinage* for ever.

From a contemporary historical viewpoint, I find the idea of the relationship between neurosis and kitsch rather significant, not least because it is based on the evil inherent in kitsch. It is not mere chance that Hitler (like his predecessor Wilhelm II) was an enthusiastic disciple of kitsch. He liked the full-bodied type of kitsch and the saccharine type. He found both 'beautiful'. Nero, too, was an ardent supporter of beauty, and possibly even more artistically gifted than Hitler. The firework spectacle of Rome in flames and the human torches of Christians impaled in the imperial gardens was certainly prized artistic currency for the aesthetic emperor, who showed how he could remain deaf to the screams of pain coming from his victims or even appreciate them as an aesthetic musical accompaniment. And in this respect we must not forget that modern kitsch is still far from reaching the end of its triumphal progress and that it too – especially in films – is impregnated both with blood and saccharine and that radio is a volcano vomiting a continuous spout of imitation music. And if you ask yourselves to what extent you are affected by this avalanche of kitsch, you will find – at least I find it as far as I personally am concerned – that a liking for kitsch is not all that rare. The conclusion that we are heading towards an ever-increasing universal neurosis does not seem to be unfounded; it is not in the least absurd to think that the world is tending towards a schizoid rift, even if this has not yet become schizophrenic, which embraces all of us, and behind which we can still see the theological antimony of the early Reformation. For the basic structure of the human problem seems to remain constant in all its various disguises, and in the last analysis will show that it is still conditioned by theology and myth.

As I said to begin with, I am well aware that I have only hinted at the problems without really attacking them. I should have said more about opera and operatic kitsch as the representative art of the nineteenth century, and I should have shown how the modern novel has made a heroic attempt to stem the tide of kitsch, and how, in spite of this, it has eventually been overwhelmed by kitsch, both by kitsch aestheticism and kitsch entertainment. And I should have referred to modern architecture, which forms the framework for all this and

42 Neurosis and kitsch. It is certainly no fluke that Hitler was
an ardent follower of kitsch.

which, in spite of this, has developed into a highly authentic art, so that it is legitimate to entertain some hope for the future. Such hopes are strengthened when we think of Picasso, Kafka and modern music. Yet precisely because of this more optimistic prospect, I should at least have tried to lay down a symptomatology of authentic art. But I am afraid that in that case we should have had to stay here discussing all night. So I am going to tell you a Jewish legend instead:

In a Jewish community in Poland a miracle-working rabbi appeared one day with the gift of restoring sight to the blind. Ailing men and women came from far and wide to Chelowka – that is the name of the community –, and among them one Leib Schekel, plodding along the dusty country road protecting his eyes with a green eye-shield and holding his blindman's stick. An acquaintance of his came along: 'Hey there, Leib Schekel, you are off to Chelowka!' 'Yes, I'm going to see Him at Chelowka.' 'And what's happened to your eyes?' 'Me eyes? What's the matter with me eyes?' 'If your eyes are still all right at your age, why on earth are you going to Chelowka with your stick?' Leib Schekel shakes his head: 'Because a man who is still fit at a hundred can be short-sighted. Don't you see what I mean? When I am before Him, the Great and the True, I shall be blind and he will give me back my sight.'

It is the same with the true work of art. It dazzles you until it blinds you and then gives you back your sight.

Winter 1950–

(Text of a lecture given by Broch to the students of the faculty of German at Yale University.)

Let us begin with an objection: if dogmatism is really to be considered as the 'evil' element in any system of values, if art should really refuse to be dominated by any outside influence, why should we not deduce from this that any form of 'art-with-a-message' represents evil? Why not ask ourselves directly whether the medieval subordination of art to the religious element was not a contradiction of the essence of art? And yet medieval art did exist and works of art do exist which undeniably contain a message, there is Lessing's didactic poetry, Gerhart Hauptmann's drama *Die Weber* (The Weavers), and Russian films.

So we certainly cannot say that all art which contains a message is kitsch, although the system of imitation – as represented by kitsch – is well-suited to being subordinated to extra-artistic purposes, and however much we may feel that all art of this type runs the risk of becoming kitsch. We only have to consider Zola, whom no one could accuse of having produced kitsch, and consider his *Quatre Evangiles,* where he expounds his socialist and anti-clerical convictions: in the frame work of a naturalistic novel he depicts an absolutely Utopian situation, which could **never be realized,** even after the attainment of a classless society, **and in which good.and** evil are not distributed according to the **moral concepts of the** future, but according to those which were valid in about **1890 and which** serve to divide people into good socialists and wicked anti-socialists. However far removed from kitsch Zola may have been personally, this process inevitably displays those dangers which are caused by the penetration of an alien system into the autonomous sphere of art; it constitutes a classic example of the action of dogmatism within a system of values. For if the bitter defence by every system of values of its own autonomy is a typical feature of our times, if this attitude, in itself absolutely ethical, is expressed in the overall conflict of values – and in this lies the tragedy of our age – the violence that one system shows to another is comparable (in anthropomorphic terms) to the behaviour of an enemy in occupied territory allowing himself to do things which in his own country would be strictly forbidden by his own *ethos.* Art has no 'personal' theme and because it is a copy, must always depend on alien spheres of values and must even draw its own principal theme – love – from the sphere of erotic values. It is thus more inclined than any other system to suffer from the penetration of foreign elements.

43 *Engagé* art imposed on demagogic motifs almost always exploits the reactionary technique of 'effect', as in this high-relief sculpture in a Russian museum.

Today, then – and this is especially true for poetry – art is transformed more than ever before into an arena where all possible systems of values meet and collide. Nor do we find that the type of art which offers a message is purely patriotic and socialist; there are also specialist novels concerned with sporting or other topics. All these factors lead us back to a common denominator, which is perhaps clearest at the point where love poetry overflows into pornography, i.e. where the system of erotic values becomes dogmatic and poetry is transformed into erotic propaganda-type art: the infinite goal of love then retreats into the sphere of the finite and the irrationality of events becomes finite and is reduced to a series of rational sexual acts.

Zola's Utopian compression of the living value-system of socialism – which was still young and vital at that point – into the straitjacket of the situation which prevailed in 1890 is no different, although less brutal. He moves the infinite goal of socialism over into the finite sphere, thus rendering the actual system 'finite' but distorting its *ethos* into a rational form of moralizing. In so doing he not only betrays the principle of the authentic Utopia which, logically, is always played out at an infinite distance, but also – and this is essential – degrades the artist's attempt to produce 'good' work to the despised goal of 'beauty'. Artists cannot, of course, be forbidden to portray socialists, patriots, sportsmen or monks, nor to depict situations which lead forcibly to socialist, aggressive or pacifist solutions (in this sense Hauptmann's *Die Weber* is legitimate didactic poetry); indeed the poet must depict these people and situations, because it is the world as a whole, in all its different aspects, which must constitute the theme of his 'extended naturalism'. At all events, to be truthful (and truthfulness is the only criterion for autonomous art) this 'extended naturalism' must not discuss systems of values otherwise than as the subject-matter of its faithful representation: it should show them in their openness, in their living growth, it should portray them 'as they really are' and not as 'it wants them to be' or as they want to be, i.e. isolated in the finite and made concrete in a way that they can never make themselves concrete.

The essence of kitsch is the confusion of the ethical category with the aesthetic category; a 'beautiful' work, not a 'good' one, is the aim; the important thing is an effect of beauty. Despite its often naturalistic character, despite its frequent use of realistic terminology, the kitsch novel depicts the world not 'as it really is' but 'as people want it to be' or 'as people fear it is'. The same 'didactic' tendency can be seen in the pictorial arts; in music kitsch lies exclusively in effects (think of what is known as bourgeois parlour-music, and do not forget that the music industry of today is, in many ways, its hypertrophic offspring). How can we escape the conclusion that no art can do without a soupçon of deliberate effect, a dash of kitsch? Deliberate effect is an essential component of the spectacle, an aesthetic component, while there is a whole artistic genre (a specifically bourgeois genre), i.e. opera, in which deliberate effect is a basic and constructive element;

44 Even if the scenery has a mark of distinction, the 'effect' in opera (*Aida* in this case) is a basic element.

but we must also remember that opera tends, by its very nature, to historicize, while that special bond between the work of art and the public, in which the effect makes itself felt, involves the empirical and earthly sphere. The means used to obtain effect are therefore always tried and tested; they cannot be increased, just as the number of possible dramatic situations cannot be increased. That is why what has already been, what has already been tried and tested, will always reappear in kitsch work. Incidentally, a walk round an art exhibition is enough to convince one that kitsch is always subject to the dogmatic influence of 'what has already been', that kitsch does not take its realistic terminology directly from the everyday world, but uses prefabricated expressions, which harden into clichés. Here too we are faced with the *nolitio,* the detachment from good will, the rupture with the act of divine creation of the world which is really of value.

KITSCH AND ROMANTICISM

This return to past history, which is typical of kitsch, is by no means restricted to the technical and formal aspects of art. Although the existence of a kitsch system of values does also depend on the fear of death, and although, as befits its conservative vocation, it tries to communicate to man the safety of his existence so as to save him from the threat of darkness, kitsch as a system of imitation is nonetheless purely reactionary. As a Utopian form of diadactic art, kitsch foreshortens, for example, our glimpse of the future, and is content to falsify the finite reality of the world; and similarly it does not look too far back into the past. We can consider the historical novel as an expression of that indestructible conservative spirit, of that absolutely legitimate Romanticism which wants to keep past values alive for ever, and sees the continuity of the course of history as a mirror of eternity. This orientation of the conservative spirit, in itself more than legitimate and fundamentally unchanged, is nonetheless immediately degraded when guided by personal motives (the personal emotional satisfaction is the most abundant source of kitsch), or when, as often happens in periods of revolution, it is used as a escape from the irrational, an escape into the idyll of history where set conventions are still valid. This personal nostalgia for a better and safer world enables us to understand why historical studies and the historical novel are thriving again today, but it also shows that this is just another way of entering a sphere that already belongs to kitsch's sphere of influence (any historical world nostalgically re-lived is 'beautiful'). In reality, kitsch is the simplest and most direct way of soothing this nostalgia; the Romantic need was at one time satisfied by chivalrous novels or novels of adventure (in which the immediate terms of historical reality were replaced by prefabricated clichés); and even today, when there is an escape from reality, it always and only represents a search for a world with set conventions, the world of our fathers in which everything was good and fair; in short, an attempt to establish an immediate liaison with the past. Similarly, kitsch technically copies what directly precedes it and the means it uses to this end are amazingly simple (one could well credit kitsch with having the power of creating symbols). It is enough in fact for some recent historical figure – the emperor Franz Josef for example – to appear in an operetta, because his presence alone creates that atmosphere of release from fear which man needs. And the same happens in the rose-coloured kitsch novel.

THE CONFUSION OF THE FINITE WITH THE INFINITE

A distinction must be made between overcoming death and escape from death, between illuminating the irrational and fleeing from the irrational. The technique of kitsch, which is based on imitation and uses set recipes, is rational even when the result seems to be extremely irrational, or even positively absurd. As a system of imitation kitsch is in fact obliged to copy art in all its specific features. It is impossible,

 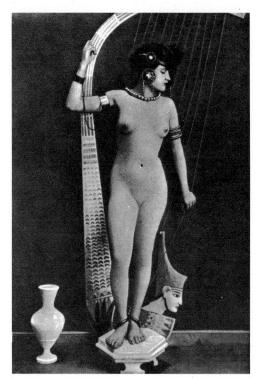

45–47 The postcard, particularly in the first decades of the twentieth century, was an inexhaustible source of kitsch. *The Fruits of Love, The Pharaoh* and *The Lovers* are three blatant examples.

however, to imitate methodically the creative act from which the work of art is born: only the most simple shapes can be imitated. It is quite significant and characteristic that, given its lack of imagination, kitsch must constantly have recourse to the most primitive of methods (this emerges extremely clearly in poetry, but also, to some extent, in music): pornography, whose terms of reality notoriously consist of sexual acts, is, at the most, a mere series of such acts; the detective novel offers nothing but an unchanging sequence of victories over criminals; the sentimental novel offers an unchanging series of good acts being rewarded and wicked acts being punished (the method governing this monotonous arrangement of the terms of reality is that of primitive syntax, of the constant beat of the drum).

If these romantic situations were to be transformed into reality, they would be in no way fantastic, but simply absurd, because what is missing is precisely that power of meaning that the syntactic system gives to the true work of art. In this system there is no longer any subjective and creative freedom of composition, nor is there any possibility of choosing the terms of reality, while the bond between the foundations of reality and the form of composition is just as illogical as the bond between a house and the architectonic kitsch inside it. It is probably the impossibility of copying a creative work that leads the system of imitation (and not only in art) to justify its own betrayal of the more elevated goal of the system imitated by having recourse to the obscure and Dionysian aspects of existence, and by appealing to sentiment. That these 'appeals' to sentiment are made by a pseudo-awareness, by a pseudo-conception of the world, by pseudo-politics or by the romantic novel, is more or less a matter of indifference; for through kitsch, any recourse to sentiment and irrationality is bound to be transformed into a rational recipe-book of imitations. For example, if the kitsch novel tries to imitate the strong bond between someone like Hamsun and nature with noisy declarations of love for the land and the peasants who work it; or if in the same way light literature tries to assimilate Dostoievsky's unending search for God, these efforts on the part of kitsch to get away from its own specific and original methods in no way cover the distance that separates it from art, and even show quite plainly how it sentimentalizes the finite *ad infinitum* (which always happens when a finite and lesser value claims to have a universal validity).

This satisfaction of impulses by finite and rational means, this never-ending sentimentalization of the finite, this gazing at 'the beautiful', imbues kitsch with a false element behind which one can sense ethical 'evil'. For escape from death, which is not the same as overcoming death, this act of shaping the world which nonetheless leaves the world shapeless, is similarly no more than an apparent overcoming of time: the transformation of time into a simultaneous system, towards which every system of values is inclined, is an objective which even the system of imitation, and therefore kitsch, keeps in view. Moreover, there is no new formative act in the system of imitation; the irrational is not clarified, the cognitive aspect is still confined to the sphere of the finite, and there is only a substitution of one rational definition for another rational definition. Kitsch cannot, therefore, overcome time, and its escape from death remains a mere 'hobby'. The producer of kitsch does not produce 'bad' art, he is not an artist endowed with inferior creative faculties or no creative faculties at all. It is quite impossible to assess him according to aesthetic criteria; rather he should be judged as an ethically base being, a malefactor who profoundly desires evil. And as it is this radical evil that is portrayed in kitsch (that evil which is linked to every system of values as the absolute negative pole), kitsch should be considered 'evil' not only by art but by every system of values that is not a system of imitation. The person who works for love of effect, who looks for nothing else except the emotional satisfaction that makes the moment he sighs with relief seem 'beautiful' in other words the radical aesthete, considers himself entitled to use, and in fact uses, any means whatsoever to achieve the production of this type of beauty, with absolutely no restrictions. This is the gigantic kitsch, the 'sublime' spectacle staged by Nero in his imperial gardens, which enabled him to accompany the scene on his lute. Nero's ambition to be an actor did not go in vain.

All periods in which values decline are kitsch periods. The last days of the Roman empire produced kitsch and the present period, which is as it were the last stage of the process of the disintegration of the medieval concept of the world, cannot but be represented by aesthetic 'evil'. Ages which are hallmarked by a definite loss of values are in fact based on 'evil' and the fear of evil, and any art which is intended to express such an age adequately must also be an expression of the 'evil' at work in it.

August 1933

(Published as the fifth section of the article 'Evil in the system of values of art' in the *Neue Rundschau*.)

MONUMENTS

Monuments *by Gillo Dorfles*

At a certain point in history monuments became associated with kitsch, (it had never previously been so) and one might well ask why this unforeseen aesthetic and ethnic debasement of their values came about, or why monuments have not adapted to the times. Perhaps, instead of evoking authentic religious, patriotic or mystical sentiments, they evoke only the customary *ersatz* for these sentiments and have suffered the fate of becoming sentimental.

This theory is one way of explaining the comic and kitsch effect of some memorial objects constructed without any comic intention; this applies to many of the great monuments of the last hundred years, from the time of Mount Rushmore's presidents (plate 51) to the recent monument to De Gasperi (plate 52), which is a genuine repository of kitsch characteristics. There is a chance that we will revere such monuments as 'La Bavaria', the equestrian statue of Victor Emmanuel II in Milan, the 'Altare della Patria' in Rome – and even the Statue of Liberty in New York. Perhaps certain funereal monuments created by artists of some note also have some claim to aesthetic value; and, although imbued with the slightly over-emphatic taste of their age, they are nevertheless interesting for their three-dimensional quality. An example is the Funereal Monument of the Toscanini family, a fine example of Art Nouveau cemeterial designed by Bistolfi. Solemnity, majesty and heroics are evidently attributes and concepts too far removed from the modern mentality because of the risk of making a fetish of them.

So, when a monument is set up in a square or park to people like the bullfighter Manolete (plate 54) or Pinocchio (plate 50) as a symbol of heroic patriotism, or to symbolize the 'Flame of Culture' (plate 56), or some Nordic myth (plate 55), its kitsch becomes traditional (like the garden gnomes) and it loses the historical content which in spite of everything lends the quality of a symbol to monumental figures.

◄ 48 The last sacrifice of the legless volunteer: out of ammunition, he throws his crutch to the Austrian invader. A monument to Enrico Toti.

Perhaps it was an attempt to avoid the danger of evoking the comic qualities of traditional monuments that has led certain artists to employ 'modernistic' styles and thus avoid the direct representation of the person or event celebrated by symbolizing them in 'abstract' terms. Unfortunately, the effect created is doubly kitsch.

Should we then give up hope for any future monumental creations? This does not seem at all acceptable. The monument is very often, even in the best instances of ancient sculpture, not only an iconographical portrayal but also the focal point of the town or city, which revolves round it. Nothing will prevent us believing that a plastic architectonic structure should be placed in a central position to function as a watershed between the various spatial directions

49 Monument to an Abyssinian campaign legionary: 'The Sharpshooters' (detail). An architectonic massif on a rectangular base 82 x 39 ft and reached by four great flights of steps.

'The great artisan (the sculptor R. R.) exulted, feeling the enormous responsibility of assuming the representation in figures and artistic symbols of the immense and epic task which is reviving the pomp of Scipio's Rome, in a rhythm of will, multiplicity and rapidity without equal or comparison. Mussolini's command stimulated our artisan from above and, like a breath of energetic enthusiasm, gave him the joyous obedience to believe even more in himself, in the living elements of tradition and renewal, through the artistic challenge for which he was preparing himself, while the classical, the expressive, the dynamic, the 'Italic', in one word were already pulsing in his veins and his spirit.'

(Fascist almanac of the Italian people – 1941)

50 Monument to Pinocchio at Collodi in Tuscany   ▶

and a focal point for views and streets. But in order to avoid the possibility of such a structure becoming kitsch, as usually happens, it might be best if it had neither a patriotic nor a memorial character and instead had an exclusively urbanistic and architectonic function.

On the other hand, every time someone tries to set up a monument which is only the empty incarnation of a non-authentic sentiment, the result is kitsch, and this effect is more noticeable if the sentiment which inspired the monument is frivolous and superficial. One need only think of the sort of monumentality expressed by certain buildings of our own time: churches, political edifices and sports palaces suffer the same sad fate as the statues, busts and equestrian monuments we have already considered. The fact that works like the Parthenon or the Pyramids still represent their age is due to the fact that they are true exponents of the ideas embodied in them. If the embodiment of the fundamental idea of our age were to be found in Victorian architecture, in the Church of Cristo Re in Rome or the Church in Brasilia, in Moscow University or the Capitol in Washington, then our age would undoubtedly be called the 'age of kitsch'. But, luckily, the monument does not count in our times, or at least counts for little: a mere charge of dynamite is needed to topple the statue of the dusty dictator or even the redundant Palace of Sport. So let us hope that in the near future none of the monuments testifying to our widespread bad taste will be standing.

51 Mount Rushmore, USA. Detail of the face of President Lincoln.

52 Monument to De Gasperi at Trento

53 Monument to Heinrich Heine at Frankfurt-am-Main ▶

54 Monument to Manolete at Cordoba

55 Monument to fertility by a
very famous nordic sculptor, in
Frognal Park, Oslo.

56 'The flame of culture.' A
monument at the University of
Madrid.

TRANSPOSITIONS

art

There are two major reasons for the outstanding popula of Renwal Art Kits. Not only do they provide tasteful, be tiful decoration pieces for the home, but building then a creative process in itself. Thousands of hobbyists h found a new sense of satisfaction and accomplishment fr hanging a completed MOSAIC or BELLE-ART project their wall. Others have taken pride in assembling a co plete collection of finished subjects. All of them have gai an invaluable knowledge of form, color and compositi knowledge that can form the basis for a life-long apprec tion and enjoyment of great art.

NOW RENWAL ADDS ANOTHER DIMENSION: TW GREAT NEW KIT ITEMS THAT OPEN THE THRE DIMENSIONAL WORLD OF SCULPTURE 1 EVERYONE!

NEW!
FAMOUS SCULPTURE KIT COLLECTION

From museums, galleries in major art centers — Renw duplicates the world's most famous sculptures with supe authenticity: exceeding even expensive plaster cast "a models" in accuracy and detail. The possibilities for enj ment of sculptures are limitless. A complete collect showcases the finest work of the centuries — for the hor for school, even for art-appreciation courses. Individual s jects make perfect conversation pieces; add a touch of gra to tables, shelves, desks or mantlepieces. And because pedestals have provisions for weight, models make id book-ends or paper weights.

No special talent or knowledge is required. Thanks Renwal's renowned precision and meticulous finishi assembly is easy and satisfying.

FIRST IN RENWAL'S COLLECTION

NO. 900
THE THINKER
by AUGUSTE RODIN (1840-1917)

Packed 1/2 doz.   Retail $4.98

Transpositions *by Gillo Dorfles*

Adaptation from one medium into another, from the means of expression of one type of art into that of another – this is an operation that often leads to kitsch. When a word, a sign or an image is used outside its usual context it will sometimes gain a new vigour, but unfortunately the opposite is usually true of works of art. We shall be dealing here with an operation that I have called elsewhere the 'betrayal of the proper medium'. In other words, it is wrong, or at best very risky, to transfer a work of art from its own particular and characteristic language into another which is not suited to it. Almost without exception this produces something in decidedly bad taste unless the transposition is made by a particularly gifted artist capable of creating not just a 'translation' of the original work, but a new work which has only very tenuous connections with the original. Otherwise the result is at best mediocre and at worst execrable. The numerous film versions of famous novels are outstanding examples of this, as are symphonic compositions adapted for different instruments, the use of themes from classical music (especially for the organ) in pop music, and transpositions from one material into another, as in the well-known case of Leonardo's *Last Supper,* which was turned into a vast window at the Forest Lawn Memorial in Los Angeles.

Evidently the bad taste which predominates in our age has acted in such a way that many famous works come to be identified with their anecdotal or extrinsic aspects, and modern man is often unable to appreciate fully the relationship between 'form' and 'content' in a work. As a result these are split up, either because attention is focused exclusively on 'form', as is illustrated by the exact replicas of masterpieces of figurative art which fail to take into account the substance of the original or its constituent materials, or because too much attention is paid to the 'content'. The latter phenomenon, in the case of works of literature, takes the form of excessive concentration on the plot and the narrative, with a corresponding neglect of the author's personal style, which is aesthetically essential, and of the particular language in which the work was conceived and executed. This phenomenon is well illustrated in literary adaptations of novels for the theatre or of narrative extracts for cinema spectaculars.

◀ 57 Rodin's *Thinker* packed in half-dozens at $4.95 a time. The three-dimensional world of sculpture is open to all!

'The Betrothed' and Co. *by Gillo Dorfles*

A typical case is that of the novel *I Promessi Sposi—The Betrothed—*
[a love story in the tradition of Walter Scott, set against a background
of the excesses of the counter-reformation at the time of the plague
in Milan]. Should this be considered as a piece of kitsch work?
Obviously not, if one knows anything about this great nineteenth-

58 *The Betrothed* on the screen. Gino Cervi in the part of Renzo with the
Lazzaretto (a kind of hospital-cum-morgue for those suffering from the bubonic
plague) as the background.

59–60 The confused love affairs of the Nun of Monza allow the novel to be ▶
transformed into a strip cartoon, with results that need no comment. Cartoons –
'I will tell you tonight, if you will show me the way to your cell and will leave the
door open!' – 'You . . . you are mad!' – **'Yes** . . . mad with desire!' – 'I shall come at
midnight, do not forget! Midnight sharp!' 'At least tell me what your name is!' –
'Egidio! And yours?' – **Gertrude!'** – 'Oh my God! Oh my God! . . . I must have
gone out of my mind! What I am about to do is horrible!' – 'And yet I want it . . . I
want it with all my heart! . . . I too have a right to happiness!'

EGIDIO!... E VOI COME VI CHIAMATE?

GERTRU- DE!

MIO DIO! MIO DIO!... DEVO AVER PERSO LA TESTA! QUELLO CHE STO FACENDO E' ORRIBILE!

EPPURE LO VOGLIO... LO VOGLIO CON TUTTE LE MIE FORZE!.... HO DIRITTO ANCH'IO AD ESSERE FELICE!

85

61 Facsimile of a page from the catalogue of the Waxworks Museum in Milan. It reads: ALESSANDRO MANZONI (1785–1873) – Born in Milan; one of the greatest Italian writers. He spent his youth in Paris and from 1810 to his death lived almost entirely in Milan, where he supported the upheavals of the *Risorgimento*. From 1861 onwards he was one of the senators of the Kingdom of Italy. His fame is due to his considerable literary productions, both prose and poetry, but above all to his masterpiece *I Promessi Sposi,* the greatest novel in our literature.
In the Museum, Alessandro Manzoni is seen in a corner of his study in Milan in his house in the Via Morone, during an imaginary meeting with the poet Carlo Porta.)

ALESSANDRO MANZONI

(1785-1873) - Nato a Milano; uno dei massimi scrittori italiani.

Visse in gioventù a Parigi e dal 1810 fino alla sua morte quasi costantemente a Milano, dove appoggiò i moti del Risorgimento.

Dal 1861 in avanti fu senatore del Regno. La sua fama è legata a notevoli opere in prosa e in poesia, ma soprattutto al capolavoro « I promessi sposi », il maggior romanzo della nostra letteratura.

Nel Museo, Alessandro Manzoni appare in un angolo del suo studio di Milano, nella casa di via Morone in un ideale incontro col poeta Carlo Porta.

century Italian novel (and anyway this book does not cover literary kitsch). This has not prevented *The Betrothed* from becoming the centre of an enormous kitsch explosion.

We should begin by stating that *The Betrothed* is not unique in this: all 'literary masterpieces', merely as a result of becoming universally famous, have had to undergo the kitsch process. We need only think of *Les Misérables, Quo Vadis, The Divine Comedy, Hamlet,* much of D'Annunzio's work, and even Proust's *Remembrance of*

Things Past, as well as Kafka's novels . . .

The Betrothed has been subjected to numerous kitsch processes, or rather has had its structure deformed countless times for kitsch purposes, and it is for this reason that we have chosen it, rather than any other great literary work, as the title of this chapter. We have chosen it firstly because the facile, sentimental, chaste, respectable, conformist and bigoted attitudes of Manzoni's work (with due respect to his literary merit) make the kitsch operation that much easier; and secondly because few other works have been transposed as often from one medium into another.

62 'That branch of Lake Como . . .' (the opening words of the novel).

The kitsch process in this case has two phases:
1) An erroneous interpretation of the aim of the work – this is a process we shall come across again in this chapter – and a belief that the novel's message should be modified. Between them these give rise to 'sentimentalization', 'eroticization' or 'historicization'. (Often a perfectly straightforward historical novel comes to be considered to have profound philosophical connotations.)
2) The novel (or tale or journal or stage version) is then used as the basis for the construction of new works, which become kitsch somewhere along the way. *The Betrothed* appears, for example, in illustrations (and is thus burdened with new sentimental or anti-historical or romantic etc. connotations which the original did not contain). Or else it is regurgitated as a comic strip (plates 59-60), as a television serial, as a film spectacular (plate 58) . . . and so on.

63 'Living postcards': the protagonists of the novel, Renzo and Lucia, as interpreted by flesh and blood figures.

64 The meeting between Don Abbondio and his henchmen

65 Lucia and Agnese talking to the Nun of Monza

66 Lucia dressed for the wedding

67 Renzo's and Lucia's wedding in the church at Olate

68 The conversion of the Nameless One (the novel's chief villain)

Leonardo and India in Los Angeles
by Gillo Dorfles

Besides the case of novels such as *I Promessi Sposi* or *Les Misérables* there are other forms of transposition which spawn works of monstrously bad taste; one need only think of miniature Leaning Towers of Pisa in alabaster and metal Eiffel Tower peppermills (plate 130). All replicas – even those made for galleries and museums – are ultimately kitsch. Think of the flood of Impressionist paintings put on the market at not inconsiderable prices not only because of their faithful colour reproduction, but also because they have the same thick paint and reproduce the details of the brushwork.

In recent times there has been a great increase in the number of reproductions and replicas mass-produced by means of the latest engineering techniques so as to 'seem like the real thing'. They are offered to their buyers complete with all the historical and bibliographical documentation. Of course one might at this point ask what we are to make of 'authentic copies' which reproduce not only the materials of the original but also its dimensions. The answer is straightforward: the reproduction, even on a large scale, of a work intended and designed for this purpose (as is the case with multiples today) is one thing; but a replica, however faithful, of a masterpiece conceived as unique, and often with a precise and irreproducible historical, religious and ritual position, is quite another.

The country in which the latter type of reproduction is most widespread is obviously North America. We have reproduced some pages from catalogues offering these absolutely incomparable pseudo-artistic wares, and have included a few illustrations of exotic monuments such as are constructed or reconstructed in Los Angeles and New York, as well as a picture of a Roman arch which we must acclaim as the supreme example of the Italian landscape in America (plate 71).

John McHale, one of the most original researchers into the social and anthropological position of contemporary art and a collaborator with Buckminster Fuller on the World Resources Inventory, has been entrusted with the task of explaining this phenomenon, symptomatic of our consumer society with its fetishization of the classical

94

69–70 Famous masterpieces for your garden, hall and breakfast room.

ITALY ?

NO...
NEW YORK
STATE!

Romance—Italian style—right here in New York State! This majestic Roman arch was built in New York's Thousand Islands by a romantic to honor the woman he loved. You can see it and a nearby storybook castle on a leisurely boat ride through Alexandria Bay. You'll find beauty and excitement like this all over New York State. Follow the pathway of history through the Champlain Valley and see Redcoats on parade at Fort Ticonderoga. Set your sails for Lake George—the world-famous playground for boating, swimming and western-style dude ranches. Relive the frontier past in the Indian-lore-filled Mohawk Valley . . . enjoy the incomparable excitement of Manhattan—all in New York State. Roads are great, places to stay pleasant, plentiful and priced right. Allow time to see them if you drive to Montreal's EXPO 67!

You'll find a world of fun in New York State this summer!

work of art and its commercial reproductions and forgeries of works of art, both ancient and modern, all leading inevitably to kitsch. 'The plastic parthenon', as he has called this chapter, seems to me one of the most shrewd indictments of a situation which is so dangerous for our society.

◀ 71 Italy? No . . . New York State! This majestic Roman arch is not in Rome: it stands in New York State. A high-point in romantic kitsch.

The plastic parthenon

by John McHale

Our emergent world society, with its particular qualities of speed, mobility, mass production and consumption, rapidity of change and innovation, is the latest phase of an ongoing cultural and social revolution. It has few historical precedents as a cultural context. Industrial technologies, now approaching global scale, linked to an attendant multiplicity of new communication channels, are producing a planetary culture whose relation to earlier forms is as Vostok or Gemini to a wheeled cart. World communications, whose latest benchmark is Telstar, diffuse and interpenetrate local cultural tradition, providing commonly shared cultural experience in a manner which is unparalleled in human history. Within this global network, the related media of cinema, TV, radio, pictorial magazine and newspaper are a common cultural environment sharing and transmuting man's symbolic needs and their expression on a world scale. Besides the enlargement of the *physical* world now available to our direct experience, these media virtually extend our physical environment, providing a constant stream of moving, fleeting images of the world for our daily appraisal. They provide *psychical* mobility for the greater mass of our citizens. Through these devices we can telescope time, move through history and span the world in a great variety of unprecedented ways.

The expansion of swift global transportation, carrying around the world the diverse products of mass production technology, provides common cultural artifacts which engender, in turn, shared attitudes in their requirements and use. Packaged foods are as important a cultural change agent as packaged 'culture' in a book or play! The inhabitant of any of the world's large cities – London, Tokyo, Paris, New York – is more likely to find himself 'at home' in any of them, than in the rural parts of his own country; the international cultural milieu which sustains him will be more evident. So-called 'mass' culture, both agent and symptom of this transformation, is yet hardly understood by the intellectual establishments. Past traditional canons of literary and artistic judgment, which still furnish the bulk of our critical apparatus, are approximately no guide to its evaluation.

They tend to place high value on permanence, uniqueness and the enduring universal value of chosen artifacts. Aesthetic pleasure was associated with conditions of socio-moral judgment – 'beauty is truth', and the truly beautiful of ageless appeal! Such standards worked well with the 'one-off' products of handcraft industry and the fine and folk arts of earlier periods. They in no way enable one to relate adequately to our present situation in which astronomical numbers of artifacts are mass produced, circulated and consumed. These products may be identical, or only marginally different. In varying degrees, they are expendable, replaceable and lack any unique 'value' or intrinsic 'truth' which might qualify them within previous artistic canons. Where previously creation and production were narrowly geared to relatively small taste-making élites, they are now directed to the plurality of goals and preferences of a whole society. Where previous cultural messages travelled slowly along restricted routes to their equally restricted, local audiences, the new media broadcast to the world in a lavish diversity of simultaneous modes. The term 'mass' applied to such cultural phenomena is indicative only of its circulation and distribution. Common charges of 'standardized taste' and 'uniformity' confuse the mass provision of items with their individual and selective consumption. The latter remains more than ever, and more widely, within the province of personal choice – less dictated than ever formerly by tradition, authority and scarcity. The denotably uniform society was the primitive enclave or pre-industrial peasant community, with its limited repertoire of cultural forms and possible 'life style' strategies.

We have, then, few critical precedents with which to evaluate our present cultural milieu. Most of the physical facilities which render it possible have not previously existed. Their transformative capacities pose more fundamental questions regarding cultural values than may be more than hinted at here.

What are the principal characteristics which differentiate the new continuum from earlier and more differentiated forms? The brief comments, offered below, are only notes towards the development of a more adequately descriptive and evaluative schema. As pragmatic and contextual they relate performance to process in a given situation. Limiting ourselves to three main aspects, we may consider: one, expendability and permanence; two, mass replication and circulation; and three, the swift-transference of cultural forms across and through multicommunication channels. All are associated with varying degrees of accelerated stylistic change and with the co-existence of a huge number of available and unconditional choices

72 Aladdin House Ltd specializes in excavated lamps which work perfectly, 'for home or office'.

73 A famous household firm offers replicas of 'masterpieces' with the purchase of a new stereo.

open to the participant or consumer, i.e., there is no inherent value contradiction implied in enjoying Bach *and* the Beatles. The situation is characteristically *'both/and'* rather than *'either/or'*.

We may consider such expendability and 'mass' replication as concomitant aspects of the same process – the application of industrial technologies to human requirements. Man has only recently emerged from the 'marginal' survival of a preindustrial society based on the economics of scarcity values; one in which laboriously made products were unique and irreplaceable.

In such conditions, 'wealth' and 'value' resided in material goods and property, as representing survival value – as ideal and enduring beyond individual man.

World society need no longer be based on the economics of scarcity. There is a revolutionary shift to a society in which the only unique and irreplaceable element is man. This is one of the main points about automation. In previous periods, objects, products, resources, etc. tended to have more importance in sustaining the societal group than individual man. Man was, in a sense, used most prodigally in order that the idea of man might survive. The material was unique. Man was expendable. Now, through developed industrialization the object may be produced prodigally. The product is expendable – only man is unique. In a fully automated process the only unique resource input is information – organized human knowledge. Automation returns value into man. Intrinsic value becomes, then, a function of the human use-cycle of an object or process. Use value is now largely replacing ownership value. We note this, for example, in the growth of rental and service – not only in automobiles and houses, but in a range from skis to bridal gowns – to 'heirloom' silver, castles and works of art. The vast range of our personal and household objects may, also, when worn out, lost or destroyed, be replaced by others exactly similar. Also, and importantly, when worn out symbolically, i.e., no longer fashionable, they may be replaced by another item, of identical function but more topical form. Swift obsolescence, whilst indefensible, or impossible, in earlier scarcity economies is a natural corollary of technological culture.

Within this process, there are relative time scales of use and consumption. A paper napkin, a suit, a chair or an automobile are, variously, single and multiple use items with possible identical replacement. A building and a painting may be respectively unique and irreplaceable. The latter have different time scales of 'consumption' but the terms of style change still limit them to more or less given periods of currency. How long does an art work remain viable –

74 'Period' palaces are already decidedly kitsch, but in the heart of Los Angeles one finds gigantic replicas of legendary Indian buildings. The *Taj Mahal* under its new name *Angeles Abbey* in Long Beach Boulevard.

75 China Town, a slice of the magic Orient in California.

76 The fairy castle and the rugged medieval style are combined in this huge 'real stone' building in Disneyland.

The loose amalgam of such ideas is often called the 'machine aesthetic'. Although claiming moral relevance this remains a 'visual' aesthetic criterion, dependent on taste. When new materials may be synthesized with any particular 'truth', surface, texture or performance characteristics required, and when their strengths and functions are at the molecular level and quite subvisible, such criteria are no more moral or true than any other *stylistic* preference.

The success of much so-called 'industrial' design has been largely through its acceptance as symbol – as conveying the image of functional modernity rather than its actuality. One might trace this from the 'Bauhaus-International' style to ergonomic tableware, streamlined typewriters and the 'contemporary' chair. Acceptance is related more to symbolic 'status' that to any rationale of increased efficiency via improved design.

Generalizing broadly on this aspect of the difference between the physical use-function and the symbolic status-function of cultural objects, one may indicate two associated trends. On the one hand, the swift growth of the museum, devoted to the permanent preservation of cultural artifacts of past and present; and, on the other, the corresponding trend towards more expendable artifacts in the present environment. We seem to reconstruct and 'permanentize' the past as swiftly as we move forward into a more materially 'ephemeral' present and future.

Linking these two trends is an interesting preoccupation with the before it is 'museumized' into a different category? What is the status of the original with facsimile multicolour reproduction? Most of Europe's main cathedrals, if destroyed, may now be reconstructed from their detailed photogrammetric records.

Then there are also the cycles of use and re-use of materials. In creating or producing, we in effect, only re-arrange some local material resource in a quite temporal sense. The metals in a cigarette lighter today may be, variously, within a month or a year, part of an auto, a lipstick case or an orbiting satellite. Such accelerated turnover of materials in manufacture underlines the relative temporality of all 'permanent' artifacts.

The capacity of the industrial process to replicate exactly by machine process, not only new products, but also, and with equal success, old products from earlier traditions, is a quality which has bothered aesthetes from the onset of the industrial revolution. They have tried to overcome this, mainly, by restricting the scope of machine process through various idea systems – like 'beauty as the promise of function', 'truth to materials', 'form follows function', etc.

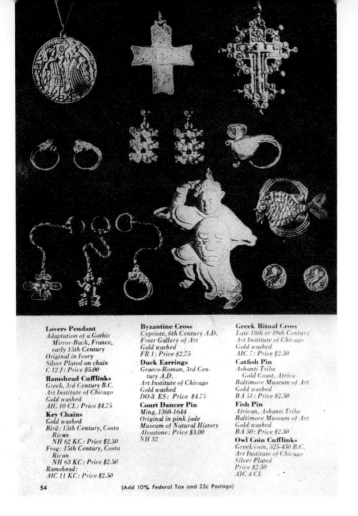

77 Debased replicas of masterpieces of jewelry, mass-produced.

'image of permanence past' which is evinced in various modes. For example, in fine art, sheer size as substitute monumentality lends an aura of permanence, or the expendable 'junk trouvé' is immortalized in bronze. Time-stopping, as in Segal's figure groups or Kienholz's full-size replica of *The Beanery,* shares a certain affinity with recon-structed Williamsburg. In the general media-continuum, the past vies with the present and future for the most lavish treatment. *Life* magazine covers the *Bible;* the movie spectacular, 'Genesis', and at European 'son et lumière' or Disneyland or Freedomland, USA, you have, '. . . a chance to live through those past moments that made our nation(s) great. See Old Chicago burn down – every twenty minutes – even help put out the fire! Visit the Civil War, and escape narrowly as the blue and grey shells just miss your wagon!'

The replication of 'permanence past' may be seen to operate in a variety of ways. Often the more ephemeral the product, e.g., fashion,

104

cosmetics, etc., the more its symbolic context is 'ennobled by time a.
by the appropriate mythological or antique image. The Venus de
Milo, the Parthenon, the eighteenth century as the 'Age of Elegance'
are used in a manner which differs from simpler Victorian eclecticism,
but depends on a reliable grammar of common symbols to evoke
responses of 'dignity, permanence and worth.'

The 'Plastic Parthenon' is a metaphorical question about the ikonic
function of sacred and secular symbols. How may we now regard the
expendable replicas of permanent and unique objects? How may we
evaluate the ways in which symbolic 'value' may be transferred in
different forms, materials and at different size and time scales in
quite different media?

78–79 Two plastic interpretations of the Parthenon, *left* 'As it probably was': a
nineteenth-century model by Stoediner, Museum of Modern Art, New York – *right*
'As we would like to imagine it' from *Classical Greece,* Time/Life Books, 1965, New
York.

The transference of symbolic 'affect' through replication has always worked for sacred objects. Replicas of gods and saints, and of their relics, carried the same magical powers as the originals.[1]

This question of 'value' is one of the central dialogues of our period. We may approach it from another viewpoint in the ikon-making function. Without lengthy discussion we may note that such ikons or 'ideal referent' images were earlier provided by local fine/folk arts, in relation to prevailing religious belief and ritual. Today, as human consciousness is expanded electronically to global inter-linkage, we may see, hear, experience more in a single life-span than ever before.

Such rapid frequency changes in the human condition generate, in turn, a rich profusion of symbolic images which enable man to locate in, learn and adapt to his evolving society. These are now con-veyed in the multiple-mass communication channels, within which we may include the marginally differentiated fine and folk arts. The constant re-creation and renewal of such images matches up to the requirements of a highly mobile and plastic environ – providing a replaceable, expendable series of ikons. These referent images of human action and experience take their character from the processes and channels which carry them, requiring no act of faith for their acceptance. Though individually fleeting, they achieve ikonic status by enormous concurrent circulation of typically repeated themes and configurations.

Secular by definition, but mythological in function, such ikons are typically of man (woman) associated with specific symbolic objects and contexts. In an earlier study[2] some major themes were identified, e.g., the mechano-morphic focus on new man/machine complexities: the rituals of the 'big' (movie) screen and the 'telemathic' actuality of the 'little' (TV) screen: the 'star' ikon and the contrastingly 'real' birth-death-life images which flow through the media channels. All the extremities of the human condition, the significant gestures and socio-cultural rhetorics, are encapsulated in a stream of ephemeral ikons, whose only constant in a pragmatic performance-relation is to immediate or projected human experience.

The speed, range and visual immediacy of such images enables them to diffuse swiftly through local cultural tradition – causing

[1] After the death of Buddha in the fifth century the relics of his body were divided over and over again, but all the same there were not enough of them for every altar in the country to have one. An elaborate system was therefore devised to counter this. An altar which contained no real relics was allowed to have instead an exact copy of one. There are many stories in which the image or copy of a sacred relic retained in full the magical powers of the original.

[2] John McHale 'The Expandable Ikon 1 and 2' in *Architectural Design* (London) Feb/March, 1959. See also McHale 'The Fine Arts and Mass Media' in *Cambridge Opinion* (Cambridge) No. 17.

equally swift changes in social attitudes and cultural forms. Two recent and extreme examples may be of interest here: one, the influence of a dime store Halloween mask as engendering a new mask-

80 A 'spectacle' which needs no further comment

making ritual among primitive Eskimos[3], and the other, a sociological comment on how the TV Western movie 'has become in Asia the vehicle of an optimistic philosophy of history,'[4] in reversing the classic ritual drama in which the good were so often masochistically

[3] Sarkis Atamıan 'The Anaktuvuk Mask and Cultural Innovation' in *Science,* March. 1966.

[4] Lewis Feuer, 'A Critical Evaluation' in *New Politics,* Spring, 1963.

defeated. This interpenetration, rapid diffusion and replication is most evident in the position of fine art in the new continuum. Transference through various modes changes both form and content – the new image can no longer be judged in the previous canon. The book, the film of the book, the book of the film, the musical of the film, the book, the TV or comic strip version of the musical – or however the cycle may run – is, at each stage, a transmutation which alters subtly the original communication. These transformative changes and diffusions occur with increasing rapidity. Now, in the arts, an avant-garde may only be 'avant' until the next TV news broadcast or issue of *'Time/Life/Espresso.'* Not only pop but op, camp and super-camp styles and 'sub-styles' have an increasingly immediate circulation, acceptance and 'usage' whose feedback directly influences their evolution. We might formally say that they become 'academic' almost as they emerge, but this notion of academy versus avant-garde élites is no longer tenable, and may take its place with the alienated artist and other myths.

The position seems more clearly one in which the fine arts as institutions may no longer be accorded the prime role in conveying the myths or defining the edge of innovation in society. The visionary 'poetry' of technology or its 'symphonic' equivalent is as likely to be found on TV, or in the annual report of an aerospace company, as in the book, art gallery or concert hall. The arts, as traditionally regarded, are no longer a *'canonical'* form of communication. Their canonizing élites and critical audiences are only one sector of a network of ingroups who variously award an Oscar, Golden Disc or Prix de Venise to their choices.

Such comment on fine art as institution in no way denigrates the personally innovative role of the artist. At best, in presently destroying the formal divisions between art forms, and in their now casual moves from one expressive medium to another, individual artists demonstrate new attitudes towards art and life. Theirs is, '. . . in effect, a denial of specialization by an insistence on the fusion of all arts but one . . . an erasure of all boundaries between arts and ex-experience.'[5] Various intuitive jumps in art may anticipate not only new institutional art forms, but also new social possibilities, e.g., Duchamp's isolation of *choice* as the status-giving, creative gesture; the development of works involving the spectator in creative inter-

[5] Daniel Bell, 'The Disjunction of Cultural and Social Culture' in *Daedalus,* Winter 1965.

action[6]. These presage electronic advances towards a more directly participative form of society, e.g., computerized voting, TV forums, polls, etc.

As the apparatus of cultural diffusion becomes increasingly technological, its 'products' became less viewable as discrete, individual events, but rather more as related elements in a continuous contextual flow, i.e., the book-novel as compared to TV. The artwork, as, for example, in Rauschenberg-type 'combines', moves towards a continuous format, juxtaposing 'still' images with live radio, and TV sets spill out of the frame into the general environment.

[6] Lawrence Alloway, 'L'intervention du Spectateur' in *L'Architecture d'Aujourdhui'*, July, 1956.

81 A famous musical: *Seven Brides for Seven Brothers*

The future of art seems no longer to lie with the creation of enduring masterworks but with defining alternative cultural strategies, through series of communicative gestures in multi-media forms. As art and non-art become interchangeable, and the master work may only be a reel of punched or magnetized tape, the artist defines art less through any intrinsic value of art object than by furnishing new conceptualities of life style and orientation. Generally, as the new cultural continuum underlines the expendability of the material artifact, life is defined as art – as the only contrastingly permanent and continuously unique experience.

POLITICS

LA VITA DEI POPOLI SI MISURA A SECOLI
QUELLA DELL'ITALIA A MILLENNI

Politics *by Gillo Dorfles*

Perhaps politics is always kitsch. Which would prove that there can be no agreement between politics and art. But it might be better to say that 'bad politics' is kitsch, or at least dictatorships are. And yet, even this is not altogether true: Napoleon was a man of exquisite taste, and so was Maria Theresa. Bad taste in politics begins therefore with modern dictatorships, and for an obvious reason: in the past, people could accept the fact that a man was endowed – by fate or by the divinity – with super human powers. Alexander the Great or Caesar were not kitsch the way all modern dictators have been without exception (even when their politics happen to have been based on reason). Nowadays, whenever art has to bow to politics – or generally speaking, to some sort of ideology, even a religious one – it immediately becomes kitsch.

Yet the great religions, the great philosophical currents, the great 'politics' of the past have inspired so-called 'good' art for hundreds and thousands of years. So what is the reason for this radical change in values? In part it is the same reason as that which we tried to define in our introductory note to explain the birth of kitsch. Beyond that, it looks as if art, by becoming more individualistic and independent from 'communal' values, has freed itself from all commitments. However much 'art and commitment' has been discussed over the past twenty years, political commitment and artistic commitment have rarely been found to correspond. On the whole, I do not believe that genuine art could have a political function these days for good or for evil. Or at least as far as countries belonging to the western brand of culture are concerned. It might well be that art could still have a political function in countries such as modern China or among some far-away African or Polynesian tribe.

Further, if a war diary, a story based on political facts, or a film, can easily be documents of great interest even on an artistic level, this will certainly never apply to monuments, statues or paintings celebrating the very same episodes as those which are dealt with in the diary, the essay or the film. Here again the basic reason is due to the fact that nowadays art can no longer retain the figurative (in the sense of illustrative and anecdotal) role which it played in the past,

82 'Go! Caesar! . . . Your task is over; Benito Mussolini emerges in Caesar, as strong and powerful as in history; his determination has a supernatural, divine, miraculous quality, something of Christ among men! . . . Caesar outlined, initiated, dreamed; Mussolini perfected, fortified, created, achieved.' From *Reincarnazione di Cesare – Il Predestinato* by Rosavita, 1936.

and therefore any attempt in that direction can only degenerate into the worst possible kitsch.

Nobody could define the relationship between avant-garde and kitsch better than Clement Greenberg, in an essay published in 1939. The very fact that this essay was written during the years which witnessed such blatantly kitsch movements in Nazism, fascism, and Zhdanovian Stalinism, merely stresses and increases its importance. We have therefore chosen to include only that part of Greenberg's essay which deals directly with the relationship between kitsch and politics, rather than using other essays, equally brilliant but of a later date and consequently less significant as far as the critical topicality of the subject is concerned.

◄ 83 The figure of Napoleon is reconstructed in a series of postcards. Each postcard reproduces an episode of his life reduced to the most vulgar approximation.

THE AVANT-GARDE AND KITSCH
by Clement Greenberg (1939)

If the avant-garde imitates the processes of art, kitsch, we now see, imitates its effects. The neatness of this antithesis is more than contrived; it corresponds to and defines the tremendous interval that separates from each other two such simultaneous cultural phenomena as the avant-garde and kitsch. This interval, too great to be closed by all the infinite gradations of popularized 'modernism' and 'modernistic' kitsch, corresponds in turn to a social interval, a social interval that has always existed in formal culture, as elsewhere in civilized society, and whose two termini converge and diverge in fixed relation to the increasing or decreasing stability of the given society. There has always been on one side the minority of the powerful – and therefore the cultivated – and on the other the great mass of the exploited and poor – and therefore the ignorant. Formal culture has always belonged to the first, while the last have had to content themselves with folk or rudimentary culture, or kitsch.

In a stable society that functions well enough to hold in solution the contradictions between its classes, the cultural dichotomy becomes somewhat blurred. The axioms of the few are shared by the many; the latter believe superstitiously what the former believe soberly. And at such moments in history the masses are able to feel wonder and admiration for the culture, on no matter how high a plane, of its masters. This applies at least to plastic culture, which is accessible to all.

In the Middle Ages the plastic artist paid lip service at least to the lowest common denominators of experience. This even remained true to some extent until the seventeenth century. There was available for imitation a universally valid conceptual reality, whose order the artist could not tamper with. The subject matter of art was prescribed by those who commissioned works of art, which were not created, as in bourgeois society, on speculation. Precisely because his content was determined in advance, the artist was free to concentrate on his medium. He needed not to be philosopher, or visionary, but simply artificer. As long as there was general agreement as to what were the worthiest subjects for art, the artist was relieved of the necessity to be original and inventive in his 'matter' and could devote all his energy to formal problems. For him the medium became, privately,

116

kept, however, within the limits of the simply and universally recognizable. And only with Rembrandt do 'lonely' artists begin to appear, lonely in their art.

But even during the Renaissance, and as long as Western art was endeavouring to perfect its technique, victories in this realm could only be signalized by success in realistic imitation, since there was

88 The Roman salute

no other objective criterion at hand. Thus the masses could still find in the art of their masters objects of admiration and wonder. Even the bird that pecked at the fruit in Zeuxis' picture could applaud.

It is a platitude that art becomes caviar to the general when the reality it imitates no longer corresponds even roughly to the reality recognized by the general. Even then, however, the resentment the common man may feel is silenced by the awe in which he stands of the patrons of this art. Only when he becomes dissatisfied with the social order they administer does he begin to criticize their culture. Then the plebeian finds courage for the first time to voice his opinions openly. Every man, from the Tammany alderman to the Austrian housepainter, finds that he is entitled to his opinion. Most often this resentment toward culture is to be found where the dissatisfaction with society is a reactionary dissatisfaction which expresses itself in revivalism and puritanism, and latest of all, in fascism. Here revolvers and torches begin to be mentioned in the same breath as culture. In the name of godliness or the blood's health, in the name of simple ways and solid virtues, the statue-smashing commences.

Returning to our Russian peasant for the moment, let us suppose that after he has chosen Repin in preference to Picasso, the state's educational apparatus comes along and tells him that he is wrong, that he should have chosen Picasso – and shows him why. It is quite possible for the Soviet state to do this. But things being as they are

89 Souvenirs, parthenons and royal families on a street-stall.

92 Mussolini playing the violin: 'Imperial power lies in the flash of the eyes. Every word uttered by the soldier, the politician or the father who loves his people is monumental; every gesture is conclusive. As a statesman his speeches suddenly become warm-hearted, he smiles in jest, and snaps out an order. He fences. He delicately touches his violin. He is at the wheel of his favourite car; he likes driving fast. He pilots his own aircraft from one end of Italy to the other' (from *Amor di Patria* by Francesco Sapori).

trouble with avant-garde art and literature, from the point of view of fascists and Stalinists, is not that they are too critical, but that they are too 'innocent', that it is too difficult to inject effective propaganda into them, that kitsch is more pliable to this end. Kitsch keeps a dictator in closer contact with the 'soul' of the people. Should the official culture be one superior to the general mass-level, there would be a danger of isolation.

Nevertheless, if the masses were conceivably to ask for avant-garde art and literature, Hilter, Mussolini and Stalin would not hesitate long in attempting to satisfy such a demand. Hitler is a bitter enemy of the avant-garde, both on doctrinal and personal grounds, yet this did not prevent Goebbels in 1932-33 from strenuously courting avant-garde artists and writers. When Gottfried Benn, an Expressionist poet, came over to the Nazis he was welcomed with a great fanfare, although at that very moment Hitler was denouncing Expressionism as *Kulturbolschewismus*. This was at a time when the Nazis felt that the prestige which the avant-garde enjoyed among the

123

cultivated German public could be of advantage to them, and practical considerations of this nature, the Nazis being skilful politicians, have always taken precedence over Hitler's personal inclinations. Later the Nazis realized that it was more practical to accede to the wishes of the masses in matters of culture than to those of their paymasters; the latter, when it came to a question of preserving power, were as willing to sacrifice their culture as they were their moral principles; while the former, precisely because power was being withheld from them, had to be cozened in every other way possible. It was necessary to promote on a much more grandiose style than in the democracies the illusion that the masses actually rule. The literature and art they enjoy and understand were to be proclaimed the only true art and literature and any other kind was to be suppressed. Under these circumstances people like Gottfried Benn, no matter how ardently they support Hitler, become a liability; and we hear no more of them in Nazi Germany.

We can see then that although from one point of view the personal philistinism of Hitler and Stalin is not accidental to the political roles they play, from another point of view it is only an incidentally contributory factor in determining the cultural policies of their respective regimes. Their personal philistinism simply adds brutality and double-darkness to policies they would be forced to support anyhow by the

93 On Farah Diba's coronation day, one of the greatest political kitsch events, this grandiose gymnastic display provided a fitting background.

94 An American shop-window where the political idols of the moment mingle with 'artistic' reproductions.

pressure of all their other policies – even were they, personally, devotees of avant-garde culture. What the acceptance of the isolation of the Russian Revolution forces Stalin to do, Hitler is compelled to do by his acceptance of the contradictions of capitalism and his efforts to freeze them. As for Mussolini – his case is a perfect example of the *disponibilité* of a realist in these matters. For years he bent a benevolent eye on the Futurists and built modernistic railroad stations and government-owned apartment houses. One can still see in the suburbs of Rome more modernistic apartments than almost anywhere else in the world. Perhaps Fascism wanted to show its up-to-dateness, to conceal the fact that it was a retrogression; perhaps it wanted to conform to the tastes of the wealthy elite it served. At any rate Mussolini seems to have realized lately that it would be more useful to him to please the cultural tastes of the Italian masses than those of their masters. The masses must be provided with objects of admiration and wonder; the latter can dispense with them. And so we find Mussolini announcing a 'new Imperial style'. Marinetti, Chirico, *et al.*, are sent into the outer darkness, and the new railroad station in Rome will not be modernistic. That Mussolini was late in coming to this only illustrates again the relative hesitancy with which Italian Fascism has drawn the necessary implications of its role.

125

95 Kennedy, Jackie and Johnson (without his wife) portrayed on 'precious' side-plates with gold borders.

Capitalism in decline finds that whatever of quality it is still capable of producing becomes almost invariably a threat to its own existence. Advances in culture, no less than advances in science and industry, corrode the very society under whose aegis they are made possible. Here, as in every other question today, it becomes necessary to quote Marx word for word. Today we no longer look toward socialism for a new culture – as inevitably as one will appear, once we do have socialism. Today we look to socialism *simply* for the preservation of whatever living culture we have right now.

96 It evidently gave the Nazi ringleader great pleasure to see the swastika on his coffee cup as well.

BIRTH AND THE FAMILY

Birth and the family *by Gillo Dorfles*

It should be clear from what has been said up to now that every ambiguous, false, tearful, emotional exaggeration brings about that typically kitsch attitude which could be defined as 'sentimentality'. We should not be surprised, therefore, if the family is particularly liable to house such sentimental attitudes.

The fact that family ties are – or should be – among the strongest and most spontaneous ties of all does not mean (particularly since it is not always the case) that their glorification and exaltation cannot be kitsch on more than one occasion.

Right from our first day of life, an equivocal and mystifying kitsch sentimentality sneaks in, pervading all rituals and ceremonies which accompany human life, from the ceremonial baptism of the baby wrapped up in lace to the first photograph of a naked child on a cushion (so often the subject of souvenir photographs), to the various religious stages of the first Communion, Confirmation (we only have to think of the serious looking boys with the silk arm-bands on their Sunday suit, of the girls dressed like little brides, of the pink sweets and all the other details of such family festivities).

But if this kind of kitsch remains within the boundaries of traditional celebrations out of tune with modern times (even a bride's dress is kitsch, with its blossoms and veil, since it follows habits and fashions of the past and is based on a myth of virginity which is non-existent today), a forcibly modern and up-to-date wedding is, if possible, even more kitsch, with the couple on an aeroplane, or wearing a bathing suit and drinking champagne among the waves, or even naked to fit in with the nudist camp (and what are we to make of parents and in-laws, also in their birthday suits, with their trembling flesh gathered in a serious attitude behind the firm curves of their children?).

The kitsch surrounding birth, like the kitsch of the various stages in family life is part of the wider category which could be defined as 'ethical kitsch'. A kind of bad taste which does not so much affect the work of art, as dress or moral attitude, and which inevitably rubs off on anything artistic or pseudo-artistic which might come into contact with it. That is why we have mentioned the kitsch which surrounds the newly born infant or the young Communicant and we could continue with that which surrounds the married couple, silver weddings, maternity, filial respect, Mother's Day, St Valentine's Day,

◀ 97 We cannot deny that the window-dresser produced some very effective publicity when he showed this king-size bed in the Sleep Center guaranteeing a happy marriage.

Engagement Day, celebrated particularly in the USA, with floods of cards which are almost always a neat example of bad taste. It is hard to believe that men have been able to wrap their most sacred relationships in such a thick veil of bad taste, dragging them down to the level of perverted rituals. From the Christmas tree to the Nativity, from Santa Claus to Hallowe'en and Twelfth Night, it is a long chain of festivities linked to a trail of images which seldom escape the mark of kitsch.

And obviously before long (and even now in fact) we will witness the anti-family kitsch, the kitsch of hippies and long-haired youths, the kitsch of addicts and beatniks.

We cannot escape kitsch: as soon as something becomes conformist and traditional it can seldom be saved, and then only with great difficulty.

98–99 Children and old people are the source of the worst type of sentimentality, which inevitably produces the purest form of kitsch.
Left An image of grannie and related poem, and *right* a composition announcing a birth with over-sentimental traditional symbolism.

Nonna nonnina

tutta bella e sorridente,

nella casa lucente

tu sei sempre la regina.

Ci proteggi dagli affanni,

resta ancor con noi cent'anni.

100–103 Married couples and marriage are an inexhaustible source of kitsch. *Top* An adornment for a wedding cake which, when opened, reveals to the amused and moved onlookers a cradle with twins. *Left* The shop-window of an American photographer specializing in 'families'. *Bottom left* The usual eccentric wedding. The caption in a women's magazine says: 'New York, March 1968. The bride is extremely happy because her individuality is unbeatable: Arlette Dobson, in a science-fiction outfit, approached the altar arm in arm with John Richard, dressed like a deep-sea diver.' *Bottom right* The Webbers, professional nudists, dance in the open air in front of the admiring eyes of their little daughter.

DEATH

Death *by Gillo Dorfles*

Death is often a great ally of kitsch, having for so long been a treasured ally of art. Think of all the medieval *Totentanz* depicted in frescoes on the façades of Gothic churches and cemeteries; think too of the baroque equivalents, even the most macabre, such as Bernini's *Luisa Albertoni* or his *Santa Teresa*, and of the hundreds of monstrous and macabre figures on French and Nordic cathedrals. We might also look, though on an 'interest' level rather than on an artistic one, at the thousands of skeletons at the monastery of the Capuchins at Palermo, at the catacombs crammed with mummified corpses and at the mummies of Venzone . . . not always pleasant but certainly not kitsch.

Today death is a candied affair, swamped in sentiment and pathos. We have death disguised as life; death concealed, adulterated and masked. All the different aspects of mortuary kitsch are gaining a hold on one cemetery after another, we have mortician after mortician, funeral parlour after funeral parlour, Staglieno and Forest Lawn and the Monumentale at the Verano (to say nothing of the notorious dogs' cemetery of St Francis). Everyone is familiar with the forests of 'realistic' mourning statues, chapels, baby temples, catacombs and modern dolmen and menhirs in certain cemeteries.

And yet the Etruscans entrusted the testimony of their civilization to necropoli, and the Egyptians entrusted it to the tombs of their Pharaohs. Death, which then was studied, respected, perhaps even loved and certainly taken seriously, is now a cosy counterfeit travesty. Thus practically all the so-called 'works of art' which multiply year by year in our cemeteries (each lauded in the local paper) are decisively kitsch. We show a few examples: the monument in which father and son, life-size, pay homage to the departed mother; the moustachioed gentleman with the equivocal semi-nude figure (an angel?) at his side. (Best not to commit oneself as to the sex of angels, it seems.)

It is sad to note that only in old, abandoned cemeteries – whether Christian or Muslim, Jewish or Waldensian – can one find some modest sacred image or some craftsmanlike decoration that does not strike a kitsch note; while the great majority of modern tombs, from the pomp of the ancenstral-style tomb with its presumptuous belief that a display of riches can conquer death, to the simple name-plates

◄ 104 The two young sons of the 'dear deceased' place plastic flowers on her monumental tomb, reached by a carpet of pure bronze.

on the columbaria (inevitably decorated with garlands or a portrait on enamel of the deceased), are no more than the bearers of a final homage of bad taste to the memory of the dead.

Perhaps the infiltration of bad taste, both ethical and aesthetic, into the confines of death began simultaneously with the loss of 'respect' for death itself. This loss of respect was on the one hand due

105 Even dogs, especially those of royal blood, live on atop their funereal monuments with the customary gaze towards the 'Infinite'.

to the weakening of ties of affection and generally to the loosening of the family structure; on the other hand it was due to the counterfeiting of death, to its concealment behind an apparently pious but in reality pharisaic mask.

106 A severe moustachioed gentleman protected by the wing of an equivocal semi-nude figure (an angel?).

By far the greatest profusion of mortuary kitsch is to be found in the country which claims to be the most religious (or at least outwardly most pious), namely the USA, while the death ritual preserves an authentic or traditionally authentic dignity in some underdeveloped and primitive countries in which technological civilization has not yet totally supplanted the primeval skills of craftsmanship.

The image of death needs vigour and severity, innocence and putrefaction, blacks and whites; it certainly needs no half tints, sky blues, pinks, angels' wings, frilly chapels or sterilized technology devoid of any real ethical meaning.

137

107 In an effort to avoid the cloying sentimentality of funereal kitsch the architect designed this 'simple' tomb with decoration inspired by Cubism and charged with extra-terrestrial symbolism.

108 The Staglieno cemetery in Genoa, in which one can find this masterpiece of funereal art, is among the richest in improbable funereal allegories.

109–111 Mortuary souvenirs, brooches (in this case with alpine flowers) and the exaltation of agricultural work are recurrent themes in the iconography of death.

RELIGIOUS TRAPPINGS

D. Mastroianni

Religious trappings *by Gillo Dorfles*

To say that all contemporary sacred art is kitsch might possibly seem slightly blasphemous; and yet this is precisely the opinion held by certain religiously and artistically enlightened monks such as Father Couturier and Father Regamey, who have been fighting for years for an art that is genuinely sacred (the former up to his death, while the latter is still fighting today). What unfortunately must inevitably make a considerable part of religious art kitsch, if not all of it, is that it is usually aimed at a public who, it is thought, ought to be fed with inferior products rather than with products of any artistic merit, for fear that anything 'new' in art may lead the faithful away from religion (or rather away from the 'old' element in religion).

In fact the few examples of 'good' religious art have not generally been properly appreciated by the faithful, for the obvious reason alluded to above: i.e. an inveterate conformism on the part of the ecclesiastical authorities, of all denominations. Even in the case of extremely famous examples of religious architecture which perhaps represent the only important artistic achievements in modern times: Le Corbusier's church at Ronchamp, Mies's church, Mendelsohn's synagogue etc., kitsch always manages to creep into the furnishings and all sacred iconological material, even if the building *per se* deserves our respect or is highly relevant artistically. This is true of the 'decorations' and furnishings of Mendelsohn's famous synagogue at Cleveland, Wright's Union Church in California or Michelucci's motorway church near Florence, and other examples too numerous to list.

Of course there are also examples of modern churches (and their furnishing and decoration) which are extremely pure and concise in their architectonic style and design; but they still lack one essential element: the religious or sacred element. Perhaps because the artist took no part, perhaps quite simply because ours is an age of total desacralization. But then would a poor and common little church crowded with typical religious trappings but brimming with a sacred atmosphere be any better than an austere and formal temple stripped of any kitsch contamination, but without any religious feeling? This problem is not a question of aesthetics and we shall not give any definite answer to it.

It is nevertheless a fact that a considerable number of the sacred images used by the church today – not to mention the decorations,

◀ 112 Mastroianni's 'photo-sculptures' have been used since the end of the century for numerous series of postcards which are still in circulation. *L'Opera di Dio (The Work of God)* is part of a religious series in which biblical events are illustrated with a non-spiritual self-assurance.

liturgical trappings and the whole apparatus that goes with sacred ceremonies – can easily be thought of as objects in lamentable taste. Even without the excesses of the ashtray in the shape of a lavatory with a print of St Anthony of Padua on it (whether it was conceived with blasphemous intent or as a 'witty *trouvaille*' in lewd taste we do not know, but at all events it is on sale opposite the Sanctuary), we can think of the countless examples of objects and pictures where ancient and sacred symbols are used quite openly in an irreverent way in anachronistic and artistically clumsy images (a bunch of grapes and a sliced loaf in the place of the Communion bread and wine); similarly we find effigies of Christ mounted in shells and mother-of-pearl where the curio element is combined with religious references; not to mention photographic reconstructions of sacred scenes, such as the Virgin and Child and so on, where the hieratic iconography of the religious image which has now become an emblem is translated into the vulgar physical charms of any old photographic model.

113 Pictures on bits of tree trunk, generally covered by handcoloured and lacquered photographs, are an excellent technical method not only for the Sacred Heart or the Virgin or the Little Flower but also for John F. Kennedy, who has now risen to the ranks of sacred kitsch.

Karl Pawek is one of the most important representatives of Catholic culture in Germany, editor of a magazine in Frankfurt and author of various essays, the last of which, *The Image through the Machine,* has been widely acclaimed. Although this is only a short essay, he has tackled the basic problems of Christian kitsch.

Christian kitsch *by Karl Pawek*

When you consider what a high percentage of the population – judging by the windows of shops selling furniture, lamps, wallpapers and china – live in tasteless surroundings, it is not surprising that the religious pictures and objects which Christians have on show are also tasteless. When you consider how bad most theatre-buildings, department stores and insurance company palaces are, it is not surprising that most churches are also badly designed. People who put up without a murmur with the kitsch in their restaurants, tea-rooms and hotel lounges should not sneer at the kitsch they see in shops selling religious articles. Anyone who has a terrible monster of a light-fixture hanging up in his home and kitsch copper-kettles standing on the window-sill beneath archly draped curtains should theoretically also be thoroughly in favour of a statue of the Sacred Heart of Jesus with permed curls. From the taste angle, Christian kitsch is merely in line with all other types of kitsch. It is equally suitable for liberals and for people belonging to the various denominations, for atheists and churchmen, for people going on a pilgrimage to Bayreuth in their Mercedes 300 and for people travelling to Lourdes in pilgrimage processions.

From the point of view of taste, Christian kitsch does not pose a specific problem. Most of what is produced and offered for consumption today is tasteless. You only have to go to just one of the furniture-fairs in Cologne, or look at the glass and china pavilion at the Hanover Fair, to see that everything has some sort of flaw in terms of taste. Kitsch is the legitimate style of the age. Industrial firms and business pools, commercial houses and cinema-owners, anyone who has something to display and wants to make a good show for his customers, favours this type of style. So churches and the faithful are simply staying within this same framework if they take kitsch into the realms of the mystical.

114 Equal sales space is given to souvenirs and portraits of the Pope, crucifixes and small Madonnas.

Nor can we put the blame for Christian kitsch onto 'simple folk'. There aren't any 'simple folk' about any more. They have risen to the rank of a universal and communal consumer society. And lastly, those kitsch pictures we were given as children were not handed to us by some illiterate donor but by the ecclesiastical gentlemen who took us for religious instruction classes. And the kitsch phenomena with which even the highest ecclesiastical authorities are involved are legion. Also, Christian kitsch is not always kitsch on stylistic grounds. From this point of view it is very often masked by stylistic traditions, garments, instruments and structures taken over from other cultural eras. But the extent to which 'Christian' kitsch is rooted in these periods which are so important to the history of our culture is another matter. The Nazarenes did not invent it.

144

Bouasse-Lebel Paris   P. F. 28   Imp. en France

*Adoremus in æternum
sanctissimum sacramentum.*

115–116 The symbols of Catholicism are clumsily represented in these small cards with a ready market.

What is unique about Christian kitsch is that there is more to it than a purely stylistic deficiency. A kitsch flower-vase does display a stylistic deficiency, but a kitsch statue of the Sacred Heart displays a theological deficiency. What sort of 'art' the Christians manage to bring off is relatively unimportant. Karl Ledergeber has pointed out that sacred art cannot exist today *(Kunst und Religion in der Verwandlung)* (published by M. DuMont Schauberg). Their aesthetic level is of secondary importance. We might allow them their Christian kitsch if this would not at the same time indicate a vast theological loss of substance, as it were. If those touching kitsch madonnas and those sweet little kitsch Child Jesuses are no longer the salt of the earth, this is on theological rather than aesthetic grounds.

145

Il Centro
Catechistico Salesiano
presenta:

L'assunta

L'Assomption · The Assumption · La Asunción · Mariens Himmelfahrt

117 The Assumption, reproduced by a Catholic organization in five languages, is depicted as a rocket in stellar orbit through hosts of angels.

This is where the argument begins to get rather difficult, for it can only be waged either with 'believers' or with 'non-believers'. A person who does not believe in Christianity will not be impressed by the 'theological loss'. He will not notice much difference between before and after because he does not accept that either of them – i.e. the Fatima Madonna or the early Christians' awareness of the Christian mysteries – have any genuine reality or equivalent in the real world. Again, believers (and I am thinking here of Catholic believers, since I am not qualified to judge anything other than the Catholic situation and Catholic kitsch) will utterly rule out the possibility of a theological loss. They will talk instead about a 'step forward in dogmatization' and will have no idea how to deal with the reproach that the spirituality of contemporary Catholicism might have been watered-down a bit.

On the one hand, discussion is only possible when the non-believers are prepared to go along with a 'phenomenological' method of discussion, i.e. if they will leave out of consideration the 'existence' of Christian phenomena. In the rest of the realm of reality, it is true, we no longer do this. Since the time of Husserl our realism has changed. We no longer have any difficulty in assuming that something exists. But in the realm of 'faith' we leave it to each individual to decide whether he will leave out of consideration the 'existence' of such phenomena. We are already making progress if we can talk objectively about the actual phenomena.

'Believers' will make objective discussion of the problem even more difficult. Ever since the Council of Trent they have been rehearsing their arguments. They will have some attractive interpretation and explanation ready for Fatima and Lourdes and the Sacred Heart. This interpretation will fit in well with the gigantic Catholic cosmos. Why shouldn't everything have its place in this cosmos, when their vision of things is so universal! Admittedly, another question we might ask is: what gets swept under the carpet in the process?

Catholicism does not make accusations of heresy, i.e. it does not cast off genuine theological substance, but merely puts it cautiously under the carpet from time to time (centuries are irrelevant here) and this often leaves room for cheap psychic and moralistic odds and ends to spread themselves. So far we have not got any accurate historical description of this process, although we are in urgent need of one to help us to understand our situation. All the same, there is a large number of scientific pointers to this today (in Catholic literature!). And many people have a deep-seated awareness and consciousness of what has really happened. The wine of 'theological sensation' as depicted by the Christian religion has been laid down in a deep cellar, but up above, in our ordinary everyday world, here and now, we are drinking lemonade, an insipid sort of lemonade, some of which is sweet, some sour.

This theological loss of substance can be seen, for instance, in the mystery of the Communion, in the mystery of the bread and the wine, the body and blood of Christ. An 'occurrence' has quite clearly been transformed into an 'object'. And yet Christ did not say: 'Carry me round!' but 'Eat me!'. That is why Corpus Christi processions are distressing today even for Catholic believers, because as well as illustrating the Counter-Reformation, they also provide evidence of a theological loss of substance.

147

We could find other parallels in the whole structure of theology. Everywhere we find the ontologically significant element and the powerfully metaphysical element (this latter phrase is a weak one invented so as to make such a conception intelligible to the non-Christian; the accepted theological term is 'pneumatology') being transformed into a psychically moral one. The vast armies which took place in the mass-migrations perhaps understood it in this light. 'Christianity' became a religion (this was a relatively unimportant step). It is not so much a question of which theological bridges were built to the new religious ideas and concepts, of whether the Christian method of buildings such bridges was in order, but rather of knowing what trends lie at the bottom of these ideas and concepts and on what spiritual, psychic, sentimental and moral level they govern the topicality of Christian 'piety'. The 'sacred heart of Jesus' can still be interpreted in this spiritual way; it is not merely a question of whether this interpretation touches on the actual Christian element, on the pneumatological aspect, but also of the type of sentimental world of ideas which this 'religious' concept encourages. It probably would not have been cultivated to such an extent (meanwhile there is also a cult of the Sacred Heart of Mary) if there had not been a sort of 'lightening' of the weighty metaphysical content of Christianity.

For the weight of our current theological concepts is always decreasing. There has been an enormous loss of substance in Christianity. This is also true of the intercessory role played by Mary compared to that played by Christ. And another question: whatever happened to the poor old Holy Ghost? It ranks far lower than St Anthony in topicality, although it represents the actual promise of Christ. But who on earth among present-day Catholics worries about the Holy Ghost? Now Fatima, that's another thing altogether! My non-Christian readers will forgive these theological remarks, which are at any rate presented in a highly condensed form. But they are indispensable if we are to make a proper assessment of Christian kitsch. It is not an aesthetic problem at all! It is not a mere concession to the people! It is the result of centuries-old watering-down of the current theological spirit and consciousness. It would not have been possible at the time of the consciousness of mystery which prevailed during the first centuries of the Christian era. It would still have been impossible in the Roman era. It was not until the Gothic period that the new psychic tendency prepared the ground for it. At any rate, it presupposes a loss of weight in the theological object, the substitution of something sweet and nice for something extremely

121 In this photographic reconstruction of the Madonna and Child, the icon value of this familiar religious image has been translated into the flat physical charm of some photographic model.

powerful, of secondary for primary, of the psychic and moral Christian event for the objective, ontological event. It was only on this emotional level that kitsch could flourish properly; and it was only where the mystery of the Kingdom of God became almost exclusively the problem of the gateway to Heaven as it worried every Tom, Dick and Harry that the 'last things' could be played down to beome mere kitsch. Nowadays kitsch lurks behind the pious statements of the preacher (in this respect most Catholics are suffering from the consequences of the liturgical movement which has made preaching a regular practice during Mass éven in the Catholic Church – this has already become a weekly penance for many Catholics, not because the parson may well be a rotten speaker, but because he is a rotten theologian). Christian kitsch is not so much a question of representational objects, stylistic factors, but of theology

118 A souvenir from Venice: Christ in plastic crucified on coloured seashells.

119 This ashtray in atrocious taste is on sale opposite the Basilica of St Anthony, as a souvenir of the saint.

TOURISM AND NATURE

la frénésie est contagieuse
à RIO

AH! les nuits du Carnaval...

Tourism and nature *by Gillo Dorfles*

Kitsch and tourism; two words which go nicely together. Why is every monument, every landscape, every object from folk lore instantly made kitsch by tourism? Why were travellers' descriptions of the pre-tourist era never kitsch, even when they were inaccurate, absurd and incoherent?

Perhaps the explanation of the *Verkitschung* brought about by tourism is linked with this phenomenon's ability to falsify and with its position as one of the most singular and degrading aspects of our age.

People who go to foreign countries knowing that they will not have to speak the language because the organization supplies them with interpreters who are sufficiently versed in the local tongue; people who travel through these countries with the sole intention of seeing the Famous Places; people who have prefabricated their (borrowed) feelings, their indignation, compassion and admiration in advance; people who take every feeling, myth, legend, piece of folklore for granted – such people come prepared.

Tourism is one of the most noisome aspects of a rite that transforms and mythicizes every event with which the individual comes into contact, once he has been drawn into the mythagogic ritual (the garlands of Honolulu, the gondolas on the Grand Canal, the Redskins of the Grand Canyon, Scotsmen wearing the kilt).

We have to ask ourselves how the tourist can possibly believe that the Indians, with their tidy, clean feathers, are authentic? How can he delude himself that he is hearing the gondolier's song or the Neapolitan boatman's song? How is it that he doesn't realize that the painter painting the Sacré Coeur in Paris is anything but a 'genuine modern painter'; that the kilted Scotsman playing his bagpipes is simply advertising's complement to the landscape?

Tourism has not spread everywhere, of course; not all the Navajos are shams, not all the gondoliers sing, and not all Scotsmen wear their kilts day and night. But we must point out that even when or if the tourist comes across authentic objects, people or events, he can, as if by magic, transform them *ipso facto* into a substitute for reality.

◄ 122 The charm of the carnival nights of Rio and their contagious frenzy are certainly irresistible attractions for the kitsch-man as tourist.

The relationship between the tourist and the environment that surrounds him is only rarely genuine, and it is this veil of falseness, imitation and admiring sentimentality that more often than not makes the world, as it appears to the tourist, vomit kitsch all over itself.

This is why we can admire the pure line of the gondola's rowlock, taken by itself, while we will not consider the gondola itself to be kitsch until it is taking tourists on trips round Venice for an 'all-inclusive' fee. Perhaps Boorstin's explanation of tourism is one of the most convincing: i.e. that tourism is no more than a 'pseudo-event', as are so many of the events which we are told about by the various mass media, newspapers etc. The tourist travels through a constant sequence of pseudo-events, with the illusion that he is admiring nature, while in fact he is only admiring pseudo-nature (the tamed geysers of Yellowstone Park; the programmed Niagara Falls; the ski-lift glaciers on Mont Blanc; Vesuvius with its preordained eruptions; safaris with tame 'wild beasts', etc). Here too, then, the element of substitution is the real key to the kitsch process.

That nature can be, or rather become, kitsch.

The question is solved when one thinks that, all things considered, much of what man creates or thinks he creates is a copy of nature.

There are, however, two clearly defined situations with regard to nature: kitsch nature, and kitsch-man faced with 'normal' nature. In the second case, the kitsch use of nature results in a 'nature' which is quite different from the real thing: and this, as we have seen, is what happens in any circumstance where one is dealing with kitsch-man. This sad individual reacts to the masterpiece as he does to its worst copy: Michelangelo's David 'lives' in the same way as its latest imitation does. Similarly, kitsch-man behaves in the same way when confronted with the finest of sunsets (when he feels 'tears coming into his eyes') or the most majestic of bays (Naples, Rio or Hong Kong). It is the most spectacular natural sights that fire him, because he can only be stirred by a great weight of 'pathos', whether fictitious or real.

But there is also an authentic type of natural kitsch, which is created whenever nature imitates itself; or rather whenever men discover the most non-authentic aspect of nature. This is true of Yellowstone Park, the Niagara Falls, the grottoes of Postumia, the Mont St Michel, and even the Dolomites and Capri, etc. The crags of the Dolomites made 'too' pink by the sun, the water of the lagoon made 'too' silver by the moon; the blue skies of Greece (or Sicily) made too deep a blue by the arch in a white wall; and the over-blossoming pots of begonias on the window-sill of an Alpine cottage . . . Even certain stones ('which look like Henry Moore sculptures'), certain dry roots (which look like abstract pictures), certain real flowers (which look false), certain landscapes (which look like painted ones). This happens whenever a natural element looks artificial: this is where kitsch, that iconoclast of authentic values, that corrupter of our most treasured experiences, intrudes.

Professor Ludwig Giesz, lecturer in philosophy at the University of Heidelberg, is certainly the greatest kitsch theorist. His essay *Phänomenologie des Kitsches,* published in Heidelberg in 1960, which Piper Verlag have reprinted in 1969, is still the essential theoretical reference for the question of kitsch. For this reason we have asked him to collaborate with this essay on kitsch-man, with special reference to tourism and nature.

Kitsch-man as tourist *by Ludwig Giesz*

The term *Kitschmensch* (kitsch-man) which Hermann Broch uses, and which has cultural and philosophical overtones, as well as sociological and aesthetic ones, is considered by many critics to be too generic, too universal, to be used concretely in an analysis of kitsch objects. It is infinitely simple to list mass-produced articles in bad taste and without any artistic value, and to criticize their faults either kindly or mercilessly. There are countless albums and anthologies which serve this purpose.

Criticism – given that we are not prepared to limit ourselves merely to facetious remarks – is generally focused on the kitsch object. On the aesthetic level, people try to contrast kitsch and art, with the following results: kitsch is bad taste; kitsch is dilettantism; it is moreover without any originality, or else totally conventional; and it is overloaded with rather primitive, affected and superficial attractions. Given that the conclusion of all these collections of comments is the same – that kitsch is not art – it would be superfluous to quote any specific titles.

Academic art-historians often supplement this type of documentation and commentary – 'some of which is arch and euphoric, while some is witty and pedagogic, and therefore culturally depressive' ('serious'?) – with erudite information on the history of kitsch: e.g. notes on kitsch in the ancient world (Hellenic miniatures perhaps, or medieval devotional pictures, etc.). All this reveals that the variation in taste over the centuries and from one cultural circle to another has been a serious handicap: when and where does kitsch begin? Let us quote the two extreme positions: a) kitsch has always existed or: b) kitsch was born in the second half of the nineteenth century (vulgarized Romanticism plus the emancipation of the *petite bourgeoisie*). At this juncture we reach point b): *sociological considerations,* and the following problem – isn't kitsch perhaps a characteristic of every mass age, beginning with the age of Alexander and Roman Hellenism in the ancient world, down to the one-dimensional man of the mid-twentieth century?

What is the relationship between industrialization, capitalism and the transformation of the individual into a total consumer on the one hand, and the kitsch boom on the other? (The mass-production

123 The tourist often 'sees' the landscape, and himself in the landscape, through the eye of the camera or cine-camera.

of kitsch articles involves limitless possibilities; the 'revolt of the masses' after the manner of Ortega y Gasset unleashes the pheno-menon of 'mass-taste'; the civilizing and cultural élites have lost contact with the public, hence the more or less unbridgeable gulf between the esoteric modern 'isms' and the prevailing taste of the general public, etc.). In this context, cultural-sociologists try to emphasize ('*circenses* . . . ?') the new problem of mass-leisure (D. Riesman: *The Lonely Crowd*), which has now become acute thanks to rationalization and automation. Even the problem which provides our title would be thrown into relief: doesn't mass tourism, with its overwhelming record statistics (1966, a round figure of 128 million tourists; 1965, a total expenditure of 57.3 billions of US dollars by tourists throughout the world!) perhaps constitute an inevitable kitsch explosion of planetary proportions? (cf. the *Unesco Courier* 1966, no. 2).

Figures, statistics, documentation – 'the facts', in short, are some-how irrefutable and overwhelming: but they are no help if we start looking for the 'essence of kitsch', motivated by nice old-fashioned reasons! For if we turn back to our original problem – kitsch-man – the existence of such nice round figures and such a vast amount of kitsch documentation does after all presuppose that everyone is agreed on what the essence of the kitsch phenomenon is. And this is certainly not the case!

As regards point a), for example, kitsch is far from being everything that is 'trash – particularly a painting' (Friedrich Kluge: *Etymological Dictionary of the German Language*, 1960).

In fact: 1) kitsch went beyond the purely visual sphere some time ago (e.g. hit-records, literature, etc.); 2) there is a lot of 'trash' about which is certainly not kitsch, but has simply not come off; 3) a pro-duct acquires its specifically kitsch quality only by a characteristic penetration, which has nothing to do with technical inadequacy. On the contrary, a kitsch assimilation of works of art does exist, but is unfortunately never taken into account as much as it should be; it must be attributed to the kitsch consciousness of the person con-templating such work. And yet we also have the equally interesting 'artistic' integration of a kitsch object by a great artist. Schubert's *Die Schöne Müllerin* cycle is a classic example: the original text was by Willhelm Müller and was composed in about 1820 as a deliberately kitsch parody ridiculing 'folk' poetry with the Romantic-cum-Biedermeier stamp! (Cf., for example, Ludwig Kusche, *Franz Schubert,* page 36 ff.) Of course, we can conveniently ignore these three points, but in that case we run the risk of falling short of the 'objec-tive', of talking of an ostensibly fixed 'fact' (because we have drawn an image or quoted a figure) without in fact focusing on the real subject-matter of our analysis, but merely on a vague substitute. In answer to b), on the *sociological* plane, we can undoubtedly observe important phenomena (e.g. connected with class culture, industrialization, the consumer society, mass-leisure, means of communication, etc.). But the limits of this way of looking at things occur at the very point where our problem begins, at the question of essence. For the sociological conditions underlying the emergence of a phenomenon tell us nothing about its substance, or even about its value. Heinrich Heine once laughed – his methodology here was shrewd – at the belief that by knowing the egg one knows the bird which came out of it.

In more concrete terms: is there any such thing as kitsch for children? (and at what age does it begin?) Is it fair to attribute a kitsch consciousness to what is known as the 'masses', who have as yet no consciousness of art at all? (and if so, beginning at what stage?) Isn't the 'cultured' and sentimental art lover and connoisseur in fact enjoying kitsch when – as so often happens – he degrades art on the pretext of hedonistic satisfaction? Questions of this sort, and we could extend the list as far as we felt like doing, must be taken seriously, because they enable us to discover the substantial limits of all supposedly 'objective' methods which are geared to the pure object as such (but nevertheless ignore *de facto* the question of essence).

Is this perhaps a start to appreciating the superiority of an analytical, apparently over-generic outlook which speaks for example of kitsch-man and does not collect ('scientifically') kitsch postcards, cushions and souvenirs, nor worry about cataloguing them?! We may certainly – like the author, for instance – not have the same tastes as Hermann Broch, or alternatively we may criticize many points in his philosophy of values. Yet we must recognize the validity of Broch's kitsch-man, even if this were to serve solely as a cue for a methodological discussion. For the 'challenge' of kitsch-man aims above all to reach that area where the question of kitsch or non-kitsch is decided: i.e. the life and experience of man. In other words, what is involved is an analysis of kitsch consciousness, which is how, finally, we judge whether a thing is kitsch or not.

If we take the example of the tourist, as we have announced in our title, this means that we intend to point out the specific possibilities evoked and provoked by tourism for kitsch-man (for which read: 'kitsch-consciousness' or, less felicitously, 'kitsch-stratum'). The reader must appreciate that we are using 'kitsch-man' in the sense of a specific inclination in man to produce kitsch or to take pleasure in it. We refer deliberately to the 'possibilities' of kitsch-man, because tourism – which is supremely indifferent to all values – can equally well provoke *anti*-kitsch reactions. The experience of other countries, (or 'exoticism') can, for example, be so overwhelming that it actually neutralizes the tourist's latent need for kitsch (a self-indulgent desire for privacy; feelings of tenderness towards one's home and family; an attempt to make every experience seem familiar by transforming it into something cosy and snug). (Classic example: the desentimentalizing effect of Goethe's first journey to Italy.) It is as well to establish a clear distinction between the modern phenomenon of 'tourism' on the one hand (i.e. a specific use of leisure that is typical of modern man and consists of spending one's holiday abroad, mostly with large numbers of people 'like oneself') and, on the other hand, the old style 'cure' (for health reasons, to cure some physical ailment), or educational travel (study-journeys with a more or less precise purpose and a specific work programme), or, again, journeys of exploration by

124 Williamsburg is still one of the most fertile tourist paradigms of kitsch. The original wording of this illustration reads: 'Not even a windy season can lessen the beauty of the historical Bruton Parish Church.' It is enlivened above all by families in period costume.

single individuals (kitsch satisfaction and adventure cancel each other out: the only thing which can be kitsch is the 'aesthetic' i.e. literary outcome of adventure: e.g. Robinson Crusoe and Defoe's

160

125 The urban landscape is often conditioned by the needs of the tourist, like this New York street.

countless successors in the eighteenth century!). As an organized system of mass-movement (even leisure is organized, as are travelling conditions and the actual resort with the possibilities of new experiences it offers, etc.) modern tourism levels out and collectivizes the psychological state of travellers, reducing the possibility we spoke of before, i.e. that of escaping from kitsch impressions.

If we study international brochures with their 'offer of new experiences', it is clear that they are directed at the kitsch-man who lurks within the tourist. It is interesting from the phenomenological point of view that advertising presupposes a latent relationship between a tendency for kitsch and tourism. Thus the offers of over-all atmosphere at the resort plus the specifically material offers are directed at kitsch consumers, often with the attraction of minimal financial outlay.

This brings us to our central theme. At this point we are concerned less with making a full list of the various kitsch offers available, than with the basic fact underlying the affinity between kitsch-man and tourism. The basically highly homogeneous kitsch curios and 'holiday *ambiances*' (which are also very similar from one country to another) can easily be understood in terms of this affinity. Our point of departure is therefore an anthropological one, which means that our first and chief concern will be with man in as much as he is the vital premise for all the ins and outs of kitsch . . .

161

I

The best demonstration of the misery of existence is given by the contemplation of its marvels . . .

S. Kierkegaard

Analyzed from the existentialist point of view, man as modern tourist is only *one* component – a particularly instructive and prominent one – of that *'divertissement'*, to use Pascal's term, which constitutes a fundamental element of our existence: it represents an escape from the real *condition d'être*, with its factual instability which, in everyday life, allows itself to be suffocated ('supplanted') with difficulty in the form of anxiety, boredom or worry.

The earliest images of paradise (as eschatological projections of human happiness, either pre-historical or historical) and the secularized 'bitter weeks and happy festivities' (Goethe) belong *before* any sociological and aesthetic questioning (concerning mass-existence, kitsch, and tourism) with man's basic anxiety, which has been expressed down the ages as the 'expulsion from paradise', 'wandering', 'travelling' (e.g. the sea journey, which appears as early as St Augustine's *De Beata Vita*), as 'intermediary' existence ('between beast and angel'), as *gemina natura* and so on. The – initially – religious knowledge of the abnormal element in painful normality (working with 'perspiring brow', despite 'suffering and sorrow', is as much a curse as the 'pangs of childbirth', which are necessary for the continuance of the human species!) still has a place in the consciously atheistic socialist Utopias of today (classless society!). (The 'proletariat', according to the most clear-headed Marxists, has still not recovered from the emotional aura of being 'oppressed and over-

162

worked'!). The Eternal City (*Civitas dei*), eternal peace, redemption –
all those ancient projections of the 'principle of hope' (Bloch) –
correspond to the 'knowledge' that our factual *condition humaine* is
transitory.

Such reminiscences, in spite of their triviality, are not in the least
superfluous to our study: kitsch-man as tourist. In fact both E. Bloch
and H. Broch agree that man's greatest aspirations and hopes lead
him into self-deception when they lose the charm of infinity and after
his over-hasty attempt to realize them in their illusory concreteness
(as if one 'had already attained them', cf. St Paul's Epistle to the
Philippians, 3.XLI ff). 'In that moment the infinite act of ethical striv-
ing is suddenly stopped, and the infinite ethical demand is degraded to
a mere cooking recipe.'

Dogmatic socialists, religious fanatics, 'pious' superstitious fetish-
ists (this already covers the crusaders) – but also tourist 'paradises'
(the most exploited commonplace in international advertising!) –
are kindred phenomena in anthropological terms. And it is not surprising that even aesthetic objectivizations (kitsch, to be precise) of
this 'blocked' seduction of the infinite resemble one another. The
Jordan water that the crusaders took home is not very different from
Berlin *Spreewasser* (not to mention tins of 'Berlin Air'!).

The motto of the plenary session of the UN which met on 4 February
1966 – at the request of the 'International Union of National Tourist
Boards' – is extremely concise: *'Tourisme, passeport pour la paix!'*
('Tourism, the passport to peace!').

Even the representative of the Roman curia agreed with this secularized assembly of the UN (April 1967)! It was known as the 'Con-
gress on the spiritual values of tourism'. (Tourism was stated to be a
'stimulus for theological progress'.) We will only state that Pascal's
Augustinian Jansenism and the Roman curia have been at variance
for centuries. However, we feel that the *divertissement* (which in St
Augustine's writings is represented chiefly by the term *concupiscentia,* in particular *concupiscentia oculorum;* cf. his *Confessions*
(x, xxx, ff.), that escapist-type divergence from one's own centre
which appears in Pascal and, as a follow-up to this, in Kierkegaard's
'aesthetic phase' and in Heidegger's 'non-figurativeness', we feel, I
repeat, that all these apply to the same essential phenomenon of
human existence, which is interpreted in the same way by Freud in
his so-called 'theory of art' (he actually gives an extremely precise
analysis of kitsch!): 'The artist is originally a man who *detaches himself from effective reality* because *he does not succeed* in renouncing

126 Australian life-savers always finish their drill with a parade on the beach. The squads and flags file past like a military review.

127 The last moment of a gory tourist spectacle for tourists; the redskins are paid.

128 Even if it is often a matter of folklore rather than kitsch, the carnival in this case presents a spectacle of undeniable bad taste.

the appeasement of the sensory stimulus in its most primitive form, and who subsequently gives free rein to the stimuli of eroticism and ambition in the *world of fantasy*. He can nevertheless find again the path that *leads him back from that world to concrete reality;* thanks to a particular attitude of his he creates *a sort of reality* for these fantasies of his to which people attribute a value, inasmuch as they think of them as precious reflections of real life. In this way, and by following a quite particular path, he becomes the hero, the king, the creator, the favourite that he so badly wanted to become, without having to follow all the vicious turns that would be induced by the *realization of effective modifications to the outside world.'* (Freud: *Collected Writings,* IV, 19). It is precisely these 'fanciful' illusions about himself and his world that we discover to be a constituent part of kitsch-man and his *divertissement!* We must admittedly limit our definition by adding that the kitsch-man is not necessarily a kitsch-producer. But more important is the fact that kitsch-man – as a tourist among other things – transforms *himself* and his *world of experience* by means of specific illusions which are nourished by the objective enjoyment of kitsch.

The examples of *divertissement* which Pascal quotes are well-known: they include every kind of artificial emotion (*passions artificielles*) experienced by our *imagination* – i.e. both in the specific arrangements connected with games of chance or hunting (including hunting hares, which no-one really enjoys anyway!), but also the part which we play in all earnestness in real life. What has this got to do with tourism? 'I have discovered that all man's misfortunes derive from a single source, namely from the fact that he is *incapable of staying still in his room' (Pensees,* 139). And the fortune of kings consists of being surrounded by people with the sole job of providing entertainment for them, thus preventing them from thinking about themselves' *(op. cit.).* The same goes for the role that every person assumes in 'real' life: 'Naturally every man thinks he is a slater or whatever, but this does not happen when he is alone in his room. The quest for tranquillity and for a lasting happiness is only an apparent one. Obstacles have to be overcome on such a quest; but once overcome, tranquillity becomes an intolerable sentence because of the boredom it creates. It becomes vital to free oneself from it and go begging for action. And similarly, when one thinks one is sufficiently secure on every front, the tedium of life (*l'ennui*) peeps through inexorably from the deepest recesses of the mind' (*Pensées,* 138).

And now, if, with this anthropological basis, we try to describe the kitsch-man as tourist more closely, we immediately understand both the fascination of tourism and tourist kitsch as an archetypal *divertissement*. We do not intend to join in the current game of *quid-pro-quo* and to consider objective factors – such as mass-existence – as the cause and kitsch as the consequence.

For 'mass-existence' in fact already constitutes, in a qualitative sense, an escape into *divertissement* (i.e. there are said to be people who, when surrounded by masses of people, cultivate and develop a sort of individual (asocial) isolation); 'mass', 'primitivism', 'childishness' – all these already represent the suppression of the kitsch problem which is uprooted as far as possible from its original basis, i.e. man. The fact that Pascal demonstrates his thesis of *divertissement* at the expense, for the most part, of kings, courtiers, soldiers of fortune and any other sort of *honnête homme* must surely give us cause for reflection? (He speaks far more rarely of slaters and soldiers.) We thus understand why Ortega y Gassett wants to see the 'mass' re-valuated as an anthropological category.

LOVE IN PORTOFINO - CIAO TURIN - MADONINA - VENEZIA, LA LUNA... E TU - TRIESTE MIA - FIRENZE SOGNA - VECCHIA ROMA - 'NA VOCE, 'NA CHITARRA E 'O POCO 'E LUNA - ROME BY NIGHT - LUNA CAPRESE - ANEMA E CORE - ROMA NUN FA' LA STUPIDA STASERA VENEZIA NO! - MULETA MIA - INNAMORATI A MILANO - PIEMONTESINA

129 Italy with its ruins and songs is still one of the favourite 'tourist paradises'. The cover of a record lists the 'commonplaces' of a traditional route.

II

Now we shall focus our attention on two favourite and character-istic phenomena, which – *pars pro toto* – must be at least swiftly out-lined in their kitsch structure: souvenirs, and ruins. The 'positivistic' index of frequency of these two phenomena is superfluous here. Our method does, however, involve taking the experience of kitsch as our starting-point, rather than kitsch objects. We have already referred to the basic pre-conditions: man's quest for happiness, his escape into distraction, which, however, – and this is decisive – does not involve either a genuine (and therefore adventurous) search for the unknown (the 'exotic') or a genuine and static tranquillity (cf. Pascal, above). Tourist *divertissement* is more a question of a pleasant 'pseudo-adventure'. We must not forget that as late as the eighteenth century the mountains and the sea still provoked a sensation of 'terror', as in Kant. For example, travellers crossing Mont Blanc had the curtains drawn across the windows so as not to expose themselves to the 'ter-rifying' view of the Alps. Haller's poem, *The Alps,* was in fact a revela-tion, in the same way that Virgil was the first to reveal Arcadia (cf. Bruno Snell, *Die Entdeckung des Geistes* p. 137 ff.) The chasm of tourism is halfway between boredom and participation, between indolence and commitment. The 'falsehood' of kitsch can therefore be seen not merely in 'idealizing' emotionalism nor in an unnatural retouching of reality – as is often believed. These are secondary phenomena, which can incidentally occur even in a work of art with-out impairing its value! It is more a question of this pseudo-adven-turous *ma non troppo* of the kitsch consciousness.

a) Let us, for example, take the souvenir, that fetish for the past. Normally our sense of time is directed more or less consciously to the present, in which we are obliged to live and work, and in which we must be constantly on the alert, because we are kept on the move by an unknown future. The only dimension of time which lies peacefully behind us is the past. The past as recollection, as past existence, is more peaceful than the headlong passage of time. The past has, for example, thanks to its conciliatory qualities, *eo ipso* great atmos-pheric resonance when looked at from the emotional point of view; it has a sort of ring to it, a patina, an aura (*tempi passati,* '*aetas aurea*').

130–134 Tourist souvenirs as fetishes of the past: A pepper-mill Eiffel Tower; a gondola with musical bells and a moving ballerina; Moscow, in the snow of course; a gaudy memento of New York; and lastly the bather and landscape at Portofino set in the inevitable globes of false snow, the obligatory medium of the tourist souvenir, even when quite inappropriate.

And so Goethe brings together the past as such and Romanticism into an aesthetic relationship: 'The so-called romantic element in a landscape is a tacit feeling of sublimity, in the form of the past, or, which comes to the same thing, a feeling of absence, detachment.' Goethe is certainly not thinking of kitsch in this passage, nor of kitsch souven-

135 The castle of Vufflens in the incredible *Swissminiatur* at Melide (Lugano).

irs. But the kitsch flirtation with the past as pseudo-eternity, and man's inability to distinguish between the past and isolated subjective experience on the one hand, and personal feelings on the other, is based on his dictum. The past is trapped within the souvenir – just as the roar of the ocean is imprisoned inside a single seashell. That is why we spoke of a 'memory-fetish'. If looked at artistically this can even be of value (cf. historical monuments and museums); but for the kitsch-man it will provoke a kitsch perversion of his sense of time. This is easy to understand from the phenomenological point of view: if my personal memory with its particular suggestive aura of past events hovers between my present (and its sharp reality) and my temporary 'exotic-past', the souvenir simplifies this sort of pleasant ambivalence by means of its tangible reality.

'Exoticism' in space and time are best integrated into the souvenir as 'mini-monument'! We should pay particular attention to the emotional *montage* of the two forms of exoticism, exoticism in space (distance, the unknown) and in time (the past, which, from an emotional viewpoint, also includes a historical 'unknown distance'). The following paradoxes will perhaps be intelligible: the ('objectively') kitsch dagger which the explorer carries when he gets back home as a memory of when he defended himself with it in a strange land is to a certain extent less kitsch than the ('objectively') more artistically valid souvenir bought by the sentimental tourist. What work of art is capable of avoiding the conversion to kitsch solely by virtue of its 'objective' aesthetic qualities? In fact, by a process which is to a certain extent 'logical', a large number of kitsch souvenirs, and indeed the most kitsch among them, are reproductions of works of art from the countries visited. Anthropologically speaking it makes no odds whether the reproduction is more or less valuable, for its 'kitsch-ness' can be measured by the place the souvenir occupies in the scale of sentimental values established by the person who happens to be enjoying it.

After these brief pointers which were intended to indicate the essential 'conditions of existence' of kitsch, we can now outline a sort of scale of kitschness. Compared to the adventurer, who actually looks for things that are strange, interesting and difficult to assimilate, the tourist is predisposed to kitsch experience in so far as he would like to treat 'abroad' as he does his personal memories: his expectations are modelled on more or less precise stereotypes, since he is certainly not in search of the 'utterly unknown'. His psychological condition is rather similar to his caravan or his camping equipment, where there is no shortage of supplies brought from home. His *recherche du temps perdu* has generally been '*trouvée*' before he even sets off; his travelling companions ensure that he will sit at a table full of compatriots, the 'attractions' of the place have already been described to him by his travel agency, and so he knows fairly accurately where he will have to aim his camera.

As far as the kitsch-man is concerned, the fascination of tourism lies in this process of the 'familiarization of the exotic', which is analogous to the privacy of kitsch delight in art (see my *Phänomenologie des Kitsches*, 1960); or alternatively in the 'exoticization of the familiar'. The two processes are generally indistinguishable and go side by side. He poses for photographs as a bullfighter, and the Acropolis is a suitable backcloth. One can even pinpoint categories of what is known as 'the study of environment' (ecology) with its distinctions between the observable world and the active world (*Merkwelt* and *Wirkwelt*), the observer and the doer, which are borrowed from zoological observation. Jakob von Uexküll, the father of environmental research, tests his theory as follows: 'When visiting the Acropolis in Athens I soaked myself in the marvellous colour contrasts offered by the columns of the Parthenon, which have been gilded by the centuries, against the eternal blue of the Attic sky, and I found myself standing next to two Berliners, one a manufacturer of braces, the other of shoelaces. Tears ran down the former's face as he looked at the columns of the temple of Athene, and he kept repeating the words: "It's too beautiful". The other, however, slipped behind a pillar and wrote his insignificant name in pencil on the marble consecrated to the gods. The manufacturer of braces was clearly an "observer", while the manufacturer of shoelaces was a typical "doer". Uexküll's typology could easily be applied to our theme, except that the two types above generally occur in one and the same person.

b) We thus come to the second example: ruins. Here, too, we do not need any positivistic legitimization of our decision to embark on this problem. These, too, are souvenirs, either in miniature or in reproduction. What we have said about 'historical' exoticism applies even more to ruins.

An autobiographical anecdote can serve as our point of departure: in 1945, shortly after the capitulation of Germany, I was asked some questions by American soldiers busy photographing Heidelberg Castle, about the history of this shrine for all kitsch-men, and I answered: 'It was destroyed by American bombs.' The reaction of the soldiers was very instructive. But I shall just make a brief theoretical observation: the psychological shock – this was certainly only an aesthetic problem, not an ethical one – was extraordinary: in their eyes the 'ruin' was no longer 'beautiful', and instead they deplored the recent destruction of an important building (thus showing a realistic awareness of the present). This represented a *metanoia,* which recalls St Augustine's puritan lament that he sinfully wept over Dido's death, but accepted the deplorable reality with dry eyes! (*Confessions:* I, XIII).

171

Günther Anders, an important critic, has pointed out that – contrary to what is generally believed – it was not Romanticism that first awakened the cult of the 'beauty of ruins'. What in fact happened was the following inversion: the Renaissance (the first generation in particular) worshipped the antique torso 'not because it was a torso, but in spite of its being a torso'. Beauty was discovered, but 'alas'

Princes Street in Edinburgh. Gordon Highlanders in foreground, Edinburgh Castle in the background.

Scotsmen are irresistible

Maybe it's because they can't resist you. They think American accents are quaint. And visitors give them a perfect opportunity to hold forth on their favorite topic —Scotland.

Fly Loch Lomond's waters on a four-hour steamer cruise (cost: $1.50); the Scotsman next to you at the railing may appoint himself your personal guide to the local legends.

Cheer out loud at the Highland Games (entrance fee, about 45¢); that Highlander at your side may welcome you into the clan. Or visit Ayrshire and drop in at one of Rabbie Burns' favorite taverns. Cost for a Scottish scotch and soda, 98¢.

Ask someone in Edinburgh the way to the Castle. He'll likely walk you there himself, to show off the view of the "new" 18th-century city from Castle Rock. He may also urge you to stroll the Royal Mile, hub of the "old" medieval city, to the Palace of Holyroodhouse—the

Royal residence. He'll be as proud of these sites as if they all belonged to him. And they all do. Scotland is loyal to the British Queen, but it belongs to the Scots. They have their own legal system, their own banknotes —and, as you'll find, their own irresistible charm.

To learn more about Scotland, send for the free 52-page color guide, *Vacations in Britain*. And see your travel agent.

Please print and include zip code.

British Travel, Box 4100, New York, N.Y. 10017

TO:		714
NAME		
ADDRESS		
CITY	STATE	ZIP

British Travel: New York—680 Fifth Avenue, Chicago—39 South LaSalle St., Los Angeles—612 South Flower St., also offers in Canada.

136 Tourist advertising uses everything to attract kitsch-man: even the irresistible charm of the Scotsman.

only in ruins. The second generation as it were inverted the 'ruins of beauty' into the 'beauty of ruins'. And this paved the way for the 'mass-manufacturer of ruins': we now arrange ruins in a landscape as if they were garden-gnomes, to embellish it! We can see how St Augustine's lament for his 'delight in tragic objects' is re-echoed by G. Anders, who has been unable to find any sort of ruin beautiful ever since Hiroshima: (G. Anders: *The Writing on the Wall*, p.214 ff.).

137–138 The kitsch paradise: Disneyland.

173

It is just this phenomenon of inversion, which was at first restricted to art, that has a strong affinity with kitsch. For the anachronism inherent in the inversion in fact coincides perfectly with the *second-hand* enthusiasm of kitsch-man, with his excessive willingness to adapt himself to playing a little aesthetic joke on the real and fleeting condition of man, with which he is perfectly familiar in everyday life: it is a matter of two or three weeks, that is all! In exchange for his money he can claim a generous portion of quasi-eternity! We can easily discover that tendency to familiarize which is so typical of kitsch-man in this anachronistic game of *quid-pro-quo* with life on earth (which is also present in art). This tendency becomes quite monstrous when even our planet is too small to be able to transform into a bed-sitter: this happened in 1965, in the Gemini-4 capsule, when the astronauts orbiting round the earth indulged in 'small talk' with their respective families. It would hardly be fair, given our theme, not to mention them by name: Edward H. White and James A. McDivitt.

With this *ne plus ultra* we have already gone beyond the limits of our physical theme – earth . . .

139 *Earth approaches:* oil on canvas (1966) by Alexej Leonov. This work was exhibited in the Soviet pavilion at the 1968 Venice Biennale: 'painters have often tried to imagine earth orbiting in the ocean of space; detached from earth, Leonov saw it both as an explorer and as a painter and he expresses his admiration for the magnificence of the colours of space and for the marvellous fantasy of the cosmic dawn.'
From the Biennale catalogue

ADVERTISING

Hathaway imports a French masterpiece: Cézanne Blue.

Most men's shirtings look positively pale beside Cézanne Blue. This striking new Hathaway color is inspired by a major French trend to deeper colors. Cézanne Blue is part of Hathaway's determined campaign for more elegant summer shirts. Hathaway's policy also includes long sleeves (noteworthy in summer shirts), French cuffs (revolutionary), and the stylishly fuller Chelsea Collar ("Dinky collars are out," says Hathaway firmly). The fabric is a very fine lawn. About $9.50. For store names, write C. F. Hathaway, Dept. A2, Waterville, Maine.

Advertising *by Gillo Dorfles*

Advertising – above all in its visual aspects – is one of the most efficient means of communication of our day: the means which has perhaps in a certain sense revolutionized the relation between the world of images and the world of reality. It is evident, therefore, that this means can be – and in fact is – one of the channels through which a message of 'good taste' or 'bad taste' can most efficiently be conveyed to the public at large. As it is precisely here that one of the greatest values and at the same time one of the greatest dangers of advertising lies (through the mass-reproduction of manifestoes, posters, pamplets, three-dimensional models etc; through the daily and periodical press, and through advertising films for cinemas and television) one can say that almost every stratum of the public, almost every age and rank of person, is affected by the images produced to this end by technicians and artists involved in this huge and varied business.

There is no doubt that the ethico-aesthetic 'responsibility' incumbent on the present-day publicity industry is very considerable, for it holds almost exclusively the one real weapon that can guide and direct the taste of the man-in-the-street; and he then becomes the real pivot of our society.

What is the use if an avant-garde gallery or an illustrated magazine for a scattered international élite is dedicated to masterpieces of modern art, if these masterpieces are then doomed to remain stillborn because they are excluded from the means of mass-communication? And yet one of the strange aspects of the present historical moment is concealed precisely here. Some of those graphic formulae, those colour combinations which were until yesterday the exclusive patrimony of the cultured élite, are 'infiltrating' today – more than one might think – into the visual message aimed at the masses. The result being that the man-in-the-street will very often be brought into contact with modern works of art – or at least with a scheme deriving from modern art – through advertising posters, film-posters, and television.

I cannot dwell here on another thorny problem of the taste of the time, namely fashion – above all for women; and yet there is no doubt that certain chromatic combinations and certain compositions used in fashion in the last fifty years have been inspired – at times unknown to the very creators of such fashions – by contemporary or slightly earlier inventions of élite art.

◄ 140 An example of facile and grotesque copyfitting in this attempt to identify the inimitable blue of a painting by Cézanne with the blue of a man's sportshirt.

Thus a Mondrian, a Picasso, a Miro, a Capogrossi have ended up by rubbing shoulders even with women's dresses and their colours, with scarf designs and printed materials, accustoming the public to a whole new way of understanding and enjoying chromatic and plastic harmony. Unfortunately, however, this modernization of taste on the level of *haute couture* (or even off-the-peg clothes) has not simultaneously been able to bring the public's taste for the authentic works of modern figurative art up to date in the same way. And this phenomenon is analogous to the one we have deplored with regard to advertising.

141 In this case too, which is in fact one of the less blatant, the advertisement succeeds in being in the worst taste; note the association between a branch of coral and the perfume with the same name, whereby the exotic connotations of the coral accentuate the mediocrity of the design.

This argument, incidentally, only concerns the deleterious aspect of advertising, only that aspect which should *not* be used and which, instead, is unfortunately more widely used than not. I shall thus not deal with valid cases of visual advertising, with those examples which are an important aid to the education of popular taste; I shall limit myself to the detrimental aspect, the aspect which is used to convey the worst elements of bad taste.

142 To advertise a stereophonic wireless that can be fitted in the dashboard, the ►
speed of a prestige fast car is coupled with the 'speed' of a piece of music by Beethoven.

MILANO-BOLOGNA
alla velocità di Beethoven

Sonar

una nuova serie di apparecchi che vi portano in macchina la musica che preferite con l'affascinante effetto stereo

Gli apparecchi **SONAR** rappresentano la gamma più completa e moderna di fonoriproduttori a nastro magnetico. Essi utilizzano le cartucce STEREO 8 che vi danno fino a 80 minuti di musica stereofonica ad alta fedeltà.

Gli apparecchi **SONAR** sono estremamente compatti (hanno le stesse dimensioni di un'autoradio) e si possono montare nel cruscotto della vettura.

La gamma **SONAR** è composta da quattro modelli per auto e da due modelli per casa. Ciò consente di utilizzare lo stesso corredo di cartucce in macchina altrettanto bene che in casa.

– Potenza di uscita 7 W per canale
– Regolazione del tono
– Avviamento automatico con l'introduzione della cartuccia
– Commutazione a pulsante della traccia di ascolto con indicazione automatica e luminosa del programma prescelto (brevettato)

– Comando a distanza a pedale per il cambio dei programmi
– Bilanciamento dei canali
– Quadrante con indicazione luminosa del programma e delle gamme radio prescelti
– Alimentazione a 12 V positivo o negativo a massa

143 The association between a bunch of flowers and the freshness of the air in a self-ventilating lavatory is somewhat grotesque.

144 This beautiful giantess in the 'fifties style fixes us with her piercing eyes.

How is one to examine how kitsch is grafted on to advertising? Broadly speaking there are two possibilities to be considered:
1) the use of kitsch material in the actual drawing-up of the advertising message, or in the manner of its presentation;
2) the use of material that is *not* definitely kitsch and that is acceptable from the viewpoint of graphic and pictorial taste, but which is used to advertise objects or aspects which can be included in the kitsch ambiance.

It is clear that I am referring to the ambiance in which kitsch-man works and towards which he aspires; the ambiance in which those feelings, ethical tendencies and social attitudes which are entirely second nature to the kitsch mentality, are encouraged and stimulated. For this reason we have a huge range of figural elements, produced in the very worst taste, which fit into the various fields which we shall have to analyze: household goods, furniture, architecture, religion, the family, etc. Elements exploited by long since outmoded

145 An example of how a traditional kitsch product can be advertised in a kitsch ▶ manner: the china statuette of Beatrice is accompanied by lines of Dante's verse.

Wiss
Jewelers Since 1848

naturale
una Giulietta
in Europerla
ha sempre
un Romeo
ai suoi piedi

Reggiseno BEATRICE in pizzo francese, con coppe leggermente imbottite L. 2.800
NELLA, la fascetta rinforzata che lascia la massima libertà di movimento L. 5.800

147 Even when there are no typical associations or transpositions a simple diminutive assonance together with mediocre graphic design is undeniably kitsch.

figural patterns, which use old-fashioned techniques, which are re-modelled on nineteenth-century stylistic plans or fake modern plans and so on and so forth. While on the other hand there is another side which uses technically and stylistically acceptable means, but which does so – and with refined expertise – with the aim of smuggling in features which we more often than not think of as kitsch precisely because they contain some of the constants of this way of life: its substitution of untrue for true feelings, exploitation of trite social clichés, abuse of patriotic, religious and mystic themes out of their proper context, and so on. There is no shortage of examples for both these types; indeed, they pursue us relentlessly everywhere: they stare at us from the walls of houses, from trains, from supporting pro-grammes in cinemas, from commercial breaks on television . . .

To give just a few examples, one is faced with the combination of a painting by Cézanne and the blue of a sports shirt, or a branch of coral and a perfume of the same name, where the exotic connotations of the product of the sea accentuate the mediocrity of the product it

◀ 146 An allusion to historical and literary names often serves to focus the attention and transform the product advertised into a sort of status symbol.

Some of your best friends are our alumni

Our students come to us from every
corner of the globe. They come
because they want to serve the world
and we give them the tools with
which to do so: a permanent faculty
of distinguished scholars; a
constant flow of eminent visiting
professors and lecturers;
access to our School of Sacred Music;
our programs in Continuing
Education, Psychiatry and Religion,
Field Education, an Ecumenical
Fellows Program and a core program
of training for the parish ministry.
If just one of our graduates has
made just one corner of the world
a better place to live, then we feel
justified in asking your interest
and support.

UNION THEOLOGICAL SEMINARY
Broadway at 120th St. New York. N.Y. 10027

Non-Denominational, free from all ecclesiastical, government or university authority, independent, ecumenical.

represents; or consider the association between the fast car and the 'speed' of a piece of music by Beethoven, in connection with advertising for a stereophonic radio that can be fixed to the dashboard of the car; or the vase of flowers and a self-ventilating toilet!

The use of historical or literary names – Beatrice, Leonardo, Michelangelo, Dante, Romeo and Juliet – often serves to focus the attention and give a sort of status symbol to the product in question (consider for example the china statuette of Beatrice advertised with lines from Dante), while references to distant and magic lands increase the fascination of a name or object (ordinary jewelry inspired by the Far East, by the Alpine star of the Austrian mountains, or by Spanish bullfights). At other times the sickly sentimentality of the

149 References to distant and magic lands increase the fascination of a name or object, as with this ordinary jewelry inspired by the Far East, the Alpine star of the Austrian mountains, or a Spanish bullfight.

◀ 148 Religious education also needs publicity; in this case, refined, international and decidedly kitsch.

150–151 Depiction of an ambiguous
object and phallic biscuits make these
advertisements – which are tolerable
from a graphic point of view – easy
prey to kitsch.

ritual of bathing the baby or the exploitation of certain of man's basic
instincts (faith, religion, patriotism) are cleverly used but almost
always in a kitsch manner. But one really reaches the tragi-comic
climax of kitsch when a famous star (a symbol of femininity and glory)
is used as an advertisement appealing to people to fight against
tumours. Even in its charitable role (warning against cancer for
example) advertising resorts, or thinks it should resort, to the worst
associations which coincide with what have always been man's greatest aspirations; wealth, beauty and fame. At the other extreme there
are countless examples where a 'good' advertisement, well designed
graphically and chromatically, resorts to facile references to kitsch
sentiments and aspects for a better sale of the product: consider the
chocolate biscuit presented under a far too blatant phallic guise, or,
similarly exploiting this aspect and the ambiguous use of the object,
the advertisement for a small massager that fits into a handbag.

186

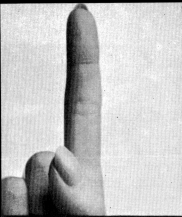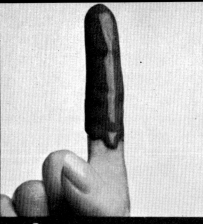

C'est comme un doigt.

Avec du chocolat autour.

Ça disparaît très vite.

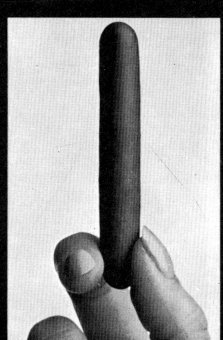

C'est un biscuit: Finger, de Cadbury.

Le nouveau sablé-chocolat au lait en forme de doigt.

Nous aurions pu leur donner une autre forme. Ronds, carrés, biscornus, nos biscuits Finger n'auraient pas été moins bons.

Quand on entoure le plus délicieux des sablés avec le plus fin des chocolats au lait, on a toutes les chances de régaler les gourmands.

Le chocolat donne envie du sablé, le sablé appelle le chocolat. C'est une recette infailli-

ble, on ne peut y échapper.

D'ailleurs, ouvrez une boîte de 32 Finger devant vos amis.

Laissez-les faire. Vous allez voir.

Les Finger sont préparés en Angleterre par Cadbury, la plus importante chocolaterie du monde. Maintenant dans les magasins spécialisés et grands magasins.

Photo by Richard Avedon   Miss Sophia Loren

Learn the seven warning signals of cancer.
You'll be in good company.

1. Unusual bleeding or discharge.
2. A lump or thickening in the breast or elsewhere.
3. A sore that does not heal.
4. Change in bowel or bladder habits.
5. Hoarseness or cough.

6. Indigestion or difficulty in swallowing.
7. Change in a wart or mole.

If a signal lasts longer than two weeks, see your doctor without delay.

It makes sense to know the seven warning signals of cancer.

It makes sense to give to the American Cancer Society.

◀ 152 The use of Sophia Loren as an advertisement for an anti-cancer campaign straightaway becomes tragi-comic kitsch.

153–154 Don't be just half a man and if you need company buy an inflatable life-size doll who will go with you everywhere!

If these features which we have briefly outlined are some of the most salient in kitsch publicity (or publicity kitsch) or of the kitsch method of advertising any kind of product (first-rate included), or of the (aesthetically) first-rate method of advertising a product that is undeniably part of the kitsch attitude, let us see what conclusions or warnings we can make.

1) First of all, and most serious, the fact that the artistic value of advertising is not determined by its efficiency (within certain limits at least, as we shall see later). Both an advertisement in impeccable taste (such as those designed by Nizzoli, Cassandre, Saul Bass, Steinberg etc.) and an advertisement in the worst taste and stylistically

189

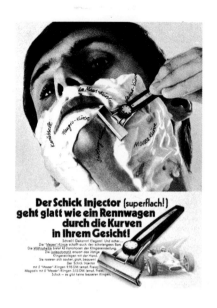

**Der Schick Injector (superflach!)
geht glatt wie ein Rennwagen
durch die Kurven
in Ihrem Gesicht!**

Schnell! Gekonnt! Elegant! Und sicher...
Die 'Meiser'-Klinge schafft auch den schwierigsten Bart.
Die Wählscheibe bietet 43 Varioffaren der Klingeneinstellung.
Die Lademsotomatik erleart das lästige
Klingeneinlegen mit der Hand.
Sie rasieren sich sauber, glatt, bequem!
Der Schick Injector
mit 5 'Meiser'-Klingen 9.98 DM (emal. Preis)
Magazin mit 6 'Meiser'-Klingen 3.03 DM (emal. Preis)
Schick — es gibt keine besseren Klingen.

155 This clumsy transposition suggests that the razor can take the corners of the face with the speed and safety of a racing car.

out of date can perform their functions. There is no doubt that the man-in-the-street is very often more violently attracted by an image that is directly related to him, an image, namely, that is adjusted to his 'bad taste'; and it is probably this that justifies the recourse made by certain (often crafty) advertising techicians to definitely deplorable images and moods in advertising certain products (moods which are 'out' from a social and worldly viewpoint).

2) On the other hand we have to admit that a good advertisement using sophisticated graphic and pictorial patterns (even avant-garde patterns) can achieve an effect that is far better than one might think. This is illustrated by a recent case of a 'bad' publicity campaign based on pictures of girls in mini-skirts bearing standards fluttering in the wind, used by a well-known oil company, which, rather than increasing the sales of the petrol advertised, lowered them because the public found the advertisement dull and unappealing because of its mawkish atmosphere; while a similar product advertised with a new type of publicity (using a style like Lichtenstein and thus taken from a kind of élite art) had a considerable success with the public and showed good sales figures, although the public was completely unaware of the connection between the style of the publicity campaign in question and the work of an established pop artist.

190

156 'Standing Out from the Crowd' is a sign of refined individuality. In this case the crowd is symbolized by Brueghel's *Tower of Babel.*

3) Lastly, it would be as well to consider the subliminal factor – much discussed today and certainly of importance – which often comes into play in the case of visual publicity images, and which is often used by advertisers – consciously or not. This factor, which is often linked to representations of a symbolic, crypto-sexual nature, is often allied with evident kitsch connotations (consider the massager and the biscuit) in showing how certain aspects of detached sexuality slip easily into bad taste; as in a verbal sense the same thing happens with double meanings, and lewd, more or less disguised words.

To return briefly to the first point, which is of the most interest to us here, I would also like to point out how the fact of pandering to public taste with artistically inferior elements, as is often done by advertising, is part of the same order of ideas that influences the creation of many kitsch works, due to the phenomenon of the styling applied to industrial objects (see page 267). It is thus a matter of two superimposable phenomena: when, in order to sell a product, one resorts to persuasive factors which are excessively commercial, and have neither functional nor aesthetic justification, one is indulging in a shameful operation, which, in the long run, can only be anti-productive for the product advertised, or for the product that is self-advertised by the anti-functional line of the styling.

157–160 Cinema publicity often slips into kitsch (even when the film is not).
Events, characters and symbols are crowded into the poster in an attempt to give
the public a complete picture of the film being advertised.

THE FILM

The film *by Gillo Dorfles*

It is not hard to see why an art like the film lends itself so readily to kitsch. This is chiefly because cinema, of all arts, is the most bound up with commercial motives, and thus almost always has to satisfy the public at large. And yet, all the same, it does not seem to me that it contains any more kitsch elements than the so-called 'purer' arts of today, and certainly not more than a lot of so-called 'modern' architecture, literature and 'consumer' music.

The most salient aspects of film kitsch are analogous to those of the other arts. Whenever the film has recourse to fake elements, replacing the true ones (fake landscapes in the place of authentic ones, fake actors, fake dialogue, fake historical re-evocations) it falls, or risks falling, into kitsch. But the fakeness can also be deliberate. More than any other art, the film has risen above the imitation and the travesty of reality. This is why the papier mâché backcloths are anything but kitsch in a surrealist film like *La diabolica invenzione*.

Conversely, we frequently come across authentic kitsch when we find ourselves dealing with the transposition of novels and famous works into historical films; or even more so with the reduction of a novel, first to a comic strip and then to a screenplay.

A great deal of cinema nowadays, then, is an authentic condensation of kitsch styles: the millionaire's house, the filmstar's bed, frothing with silk, the pretentious hotel, the café-society dandy. In these cases we are not quite sure whether to consider the film as an authentic documentary showing the costume of the time or as a collection of skilfully displayed kitsch elements.

And in my opinion the kitsch element in great historical and legendary screen hits like *The Fire of Rome, A Thousand and One Nights, Nero, The Nibelungs* or in mock heroic films (Maciste, Ursus, Tarzan) is too explicit to require any kind of critical comment.

No other cinema historian is better qualified to write on kitsch in the film than Lotte H. Eisner, author of the well-known *Schermo Demoniaco* and of numerous other essays. Her Germanic culture and her extensive knowledge of the vast amount of material in her charge at the Cinémathèque Française, are the basis of this essay on kitsch in the cinema, which deserves more space.

◀ 161 The depiction of a famous painter on the screen is painful even in the hands of a director with taste. Vincente Minnelli's film about van Gogh, *Lust for Life* (1956).

162 Maciste lifts a papier mâché boulder in his comic-heroic struggle against the monsters.

Kitsch in the cinema *by Lotte H. Eisner*

One might therefore think that the essential characteristic of kitsch really consists of its appeal to the indestructible reactionary ferments of man. The combination of kitsch elements will at all events be different for every age.

HERBERT IHERING *The 'Twenties*
(Aufbau Verlag, Berlin 1948)

The definition of kitsch in the cinema is far less rigid and infinitely less consistent than in any other type of figurative art. The difficulty perhaps lies in the fact that in this case one is not dealing with a fixed image to which one can refer again to confirm one's assertions; a frame leaves only a fleeting impression and is quickly replaced by the next frame as the events are narrated.

Where painting is concerned a picture is kitsch a priori; or, as in the case of Hans Makart, it can express the quintessence of beauty in the eyes of one generation and be rejected as kitsch by the next.

Different considerations are involved where the cinema is concerned. Kitsch, as an obvious maxim has it, 'is in the eye of the beholder'. If I had gone to the cinema in 1914-15, I would certainly have thought of the films full of army uniforms and patriotism, or films like *Liebesglück der Blinden* with Henny Porten as kitsch.

Six years later people would find some way of rehabilitating them as 'contemporary documents'. For in the meantime they would have become expressions of their age, of historical interest to the sociologist and the film historian alike. Both from the angle of social criticism and from the point of view of costume, these films are nowadays considered to be valuable 'primitive' examples of what is known as 'naïve art'. They have a kind of patina and we would like to have rescued and preserved them.

This may also be true of a large number of paintings. How can we know what future generations will see in certain paintings by Bocklin, which were the pride of bourgeois homes at the turn of the century, in the smoothly stylized work of Stuck or in the pseudo-modern painter Hodler.

To begin with, the Cinémathèque Française concentrated on collecting historical films or films with 'artistic' merit. That tireless collector Henri Langlois rapidly abandoned this criterion and eventually accepted every film offered to him, even really 'ham' ones, which are known in French as *navets*. He stresses that we cannot arbitrarily limit ourselves to collecting only those films which seem to us now to be of value. In ten, twenty or thirty years, a new generation may, for one reason or another, find a film extremely interesting which seems to us today utterly atrocious.

I have experienced this myself, first as an art historian and later as a film-critic. Towards the end of the 'twenties I went to a retrospective showing of Fritz Lang's *Nibelungen* (plate 163) which I found very 'Teutonic' and the lovers beneath the tree in full bloom struck me as very kitsch. Similarly, all the idling about in the gardens of the rich, the dance by the false Mary and the ecstatic swoon of the young Freder as he kneels before the real Mary in Lang's *Metropolis* (1926) also seemed kitsch.

But when I saw these films again forty years later I realized that sequences like these were for the most part typical examples of 'Viennese' or 'Munich' industrial art – introduced into the cinema some ten or fifteen years later than other art forms which are always ahead of the cinema, as with Caligari and Expressionism. I realized, on the other hand, that the exaggeratedly soulful element in the films of Abel Gance, Marcel l'Herbier or Fritz Lang during the 'twenties were typical of the excessive sentimentality which made its appearance after the First World War.

The same goes for those flowery sub-titles and poetic commentaries in the films of D. W. Griffith, Gance or l'Herbier which make us smile today.

The affectation of F. W. Murnau's *Faust* (1926) must also be understood in this light. Here too, though, as in the other films quoted, there are some superb sequences which give so much enjoyment that the incriminating scenes hardly jar on us at all; indeed, for a generation which looks at things more realistically, they become a remarkable expression of the sentiments of the age.

163 A still taken from Fritz Lang's *Nibelungen* might give a mistaken ▶
impression of kitsch. The excessive sentimentality is a consequence of the First
World War and is not necessarily kitsch, just as the characteristics of industrial
art do not mean (in this case) kitsch.

164 A still from Anton Giulio Bragaglia's *Perfido Incanto* (1916): the conscious realization of futurist principles eliminates any possibility of kitsch.

It should, moreover, be significant that there is no trace of kitsch in films which follow unequivocally Futuristic or Expressionistic precepts, because nowhere in such films can we detect a definite stylistic break. Good evidence of this can be seen in J. C. Bragaglia's *Perfido incanto* (1916) (plate 164) and Robert Wiene's *Das Kabinett des Dr Caligari* (1919).

According to the definition in Knaur's Encyclopedia 'kitsch' is a realization of artistic motifs falsified by stylistic hypersentimentality or inadequacy.

We have been able to see that a hypersentimental film does not need to be translated into kitsch terms by looking at the films of Gance and l'Herbier in the French cinema and Lang or Murnau in the German cinema. The same is true of the precious poses and affected gestures of the *diva* in the Italian cinema between 1910 and 1930. Pina Menichelli (plate 165) is never kitsch, despite the inordinate

200

165 A still with Pina Menichelli in Pastrone's *Fuoco* (1915). The gyration of the *diva's* attitudes is not necessarily kitsch.

exaggeration of her supple panther-like movements and her voluptuous writhing; in Patrone's *Fuoco* (1915) and elsewhere, she embodies the quintessence of Gabriele d'Annunzio's mysterious heroines.

Pastrone's *Tigre reale* (1916), Nino Oxilio's *Il giardino della volutta* (1918) or his *Rapsodia satanica* (1915) with Lyda Borelli are mirrors of their age, the expression of an outlook which is at times very different from ours and perhaps not always intelligible to us.

So kitsch in the cinema is a different matter. If we want to understand it we must call on another German term—'*Stimmung*'—which is as untranslateable as *kitsch* and has become an integrating factor in the cinema. *Stimmung,* especially in the French and German cinema, means both '*atmosphère*' and '*ambiance*' in French, in English '*mood*', in Italian something like '*intonazione*' or '*ambiente*', but none of these terms can do full justice to the word. '*Intonazione*' does perhaps evoke something of the infinitely musical chord of *'Stimmung'* which Novalis speaks of, but it certainly does not provide an exact interpretation of the whole meaning of the term. A film either has an authentic *'Stimmung'* or an artificial and false one: the *Stimmung* of the various scenes in E. A. Dupont's film *Das Alte Gesetz* (1924) is austere, simple and genuinely poetic.

The artificial *Stimmung* in Joe May's *Heimkehr* (1928), with its exaggeratedly sophisticated chiaroscuro, and its affected sfumato which blurs the outlines, becomes characteristic of what is known as the reactionary *'Ufastil'* in the late 'twenties; it becomes the mark of all the later Nazi films in period costume.

So this is where we find that falsified 'artistic' work which Knaur's Encyclopedia talks about.

In a world as rich in false values as the Nazi world, with all the false sentimentality of *'Blut und Boden'* (blood and earth) or *'Kraft durch Freude'* (strength through joy), kitsch becomes a matter of course.

166 The attitude of Lyda Borelli in *Rapsodia Satanica* by Nino Oxilia (1915) is the expression of an age and mentality which are both far removed from our own day and are susceptible of ambiguous verdicts.

Chiaroscuro, a relic of Expressionism, is demoted to an affected *'grisaille'* which is imposed on the cameramen, reliefs lose their force and are faded, volumes become indeterminate and lose their plastic quality. And all this in spite of Goebbels's statement that he wanted films made 'with strong popular outlines', a milieu and people corresponding to the real world.

Thus the fatal idealization of blond Germanic beauty, exalted in a still from Steinhoff's *Hitlerjunge Quex* (1933) (plate 167).

167 'Blond beauty' kitsch. Hans Steinhoff's *Hitlerjunge Quex* (1933).

This glorification of blond beauty is not a completely new phenomenon, however. Alongside the small number of films which are nowadays thought of as classics, Germany has always produced a flood of mediocre films for the masses. The *Heimatfilm* which exalts the forests and meadows of Germany and her simple folk, in which Paul Richter – Fritz Lang's Siegfried – played the rough and vigorous gamekeeper, existed long before Nazi ideology and continued to flourish in the post-Hitler period, because the general public hated the famous *Trümmerfilme* (débris films) which tell of the downfall of Germany.

This is the time when the ingenious German distributors of one of Truffaut's films *Les quatre cents coups* (1959) – which should logically have been called *Flegeljahre* (The years of puberty), were to invent long kitsch titles: *Sie küssten ihn und schlugen ihn* (They kissed him and beat him).

Die Heilige und ihr Narr (The Saint and her Simpleton) (plate 168), a kitsch novel gushing with affectation, was adapted for the screen as early as 1928 by Wilhelm Dieterle (now William Dieterle in the USA). This film illustrates the same fatal mania for blond beauty and equivocal innocence.

This mania is not of course exclusive to the German cinema; the false folklore of many American films forms a pendant to this type of kitsch scene: a good example of this is Robert Z. Leonard's *Maytime* (1937) (plate 169) a musical with a cast of farmers and farm-girls quite removed from reality and the usual blossoming trees, in which there is, alas, no trace of any Stroheim-like irony. But the allegedly 'genuine' Russian-ness of *The End of the Rainbow* (1947) by Allan Dwann (plate 170) has an even more disastrous effect, even if the extras were in fact played by real *émigrés* in their original costumes.

168 An equivocal and affected innocence becomes kitsch. W. Dieterle's *Die Heilige und ihr Narr* (1928)

169–170 *Right* Fake folklore kitsch in the USA. Robert Z. Leonard's *Maytime* (1937) and the *End of the Rainbow* by Allan Dwan (1947).

There is an analogy between the German cinema of the Nazi period and the Italian cinema under the Fascist regime. This is the era of the 'white telephone', of a falsely elegant social milieu to which most of the directors of the time unfortunately paid homage.

We can thus fairly say that kitsch corresponds at least partly to a reactionary attitude.

Above we have illustrated false *Stimmung* but we also find false subjects. It is almost always painful to see famous people on the screen. It is painful to see a Napoleon who is too tall: Charles Boyer in Clarence Brown's *Maria Valeska* (1938) has to walk bent double. It is painful to think of José Ferrer, since we can never forget that he had to walk on his knees when he played Toulouse-Lautrec in John Huston's *Moulin Rouge*. It is even painful to see Modigliani in Jacques Becker's *Montparnesse 19* (1957) even though he is played by a great actor like Gérard Philipe and directed by someone as good as Becker. The same goes for Kirk Douglas as Van Gogh painting his famous picture, even though the film is discreetly directed by a tasteful director like Vincente Minnelli (plate 161).

However, these examples are not really quite kitsch. If the Van Gogh film dealt instead with an anonymous Mr X, we would have no reason to feel shocked by the development of the story. The danger lies in the excessive emphasis laid on fame. In this way we lose the immediacy of a personality as it exists in our mind's eye. We are forced into make-believe, and as with a day-dream we remain totally passive. We have the feeling that we are looking at wax figures which are driven along like automatons by some invisible machinery. Even when Abel Gance, that Victor Hugo of the cinema, does achieve some moments of stirring ecstasy in his *Un grand amour de Beethoven* (1936), or when a great actor like Jean-Louis Barrault manages to make his Berlioz really three-dimensional in the *Symphonie fantastique* (1942) (plate 37), the feeling that these are plaster figures is still there.

It suffices to contrast these films with films based on authentic documentary material of the lives of great painters – for example *Le mystère Picasso* (1956) by Clouzot, or Jean Gremillon's *André Masson et les quatre éléments* (1958) – to realize that the mystery of the creative moment is suggested and explained here, the mystery of the direct and immediate revelation of genius. It is precisely this that holds us and takes our breath away.

This makes us aware of the substitute, the kitsch element – the make-up, the wigs, the costumes from some secondhand clothes shop – in commercial films about artists, which have analogies with the

206

living tableaux in nineteenth-century soirées. We should especially beware of films dedicated to great musicians which have been flourishing ever since the sound film first made its appearance, with the love-life of great composers and an inevitable flood of *Lieder*, particularly the most unfortunate films about Schubert, such as Willy Forst's playful *Dreimäderlhaus* or *Leise flehen meine Lieder* (1933) (plate 172), both German, or their English counterpart, Paul Ludwig Stein's *Blossom Time* (1934) in which Hans Jarosy and the tenor Richard Tauber had the same faces, which were ostensibly 'exact' replicas of Schubert's death mask. But still less acceptable is a young

171 The young Beethoven at the piano in Georg Tressler's *Magnificent Rebel* (USA, 1961).

Beethoven with false eyelashes, played by a mediocre actor with a broad face who sat at the piano in Georg Tressler's *The Magnificent Rebel* (1961) (plate 171) and even worse, a young Rembrandt sitting at

207

172 A popular film about Schubert with an actor strongly resembling the musician immediately becomes kitsch. Willy Forst's *Leise flehen meine Leider* (1933).

his easel in Steinhoff's insulting *Rembrandt* (plate 173) which dates from 1942, i.e. the Nazi period.

What is really important, at all events is *how* a film has been made and not *what* it relates. We follow the events narrated in Abel Gance's first *Napoleon* (1926) with bated breath, even though the young Bonaparte is played by a not particularly good actor, Albert Dieudonné.

208

173 Young Rembrandt at his easel in Steinhoff's insulting *Rembrandt* made in the Nazi period (as may be seen from the stamp on the photograph).

In Gance's films an authentic heroism predominates, pathos in the real sense of the word. What distorts our image of a famous person is primarily the banal situation.

It would be unfair to raise the objection that in Gance's case we are dealing with a 'twenties classic. Lupu Pick's *Napoleon auf Sankt Helena* (1928) – Pick has in fact made two well-known chamber music films *Scherben* (1921) and *Sylvester* (1923) – is dry and lifeless in comparison; it is the sort of 'constructed account' that leads to kitsch.

174 The genesis of the film *Cleopatra*. One of the first was with Theda Bara (1917). Kitsch becomes more perceptible in the foreground.

175 *Cleopatra* as a revue, made by Cecil B. de Mille, with Claudette Colbert.

176 A more modern Cleopatra in the shape of Elizabeth Taylor in the film by Joseph L. Mankiewicz (1962).

Even if we might think of J. E. Edwards *Cleopatra* (1917) with the vamp Theda Bara (plate 174) as historically valuable, we cannot deny that the supposedly Egyptian gesture of the arms achieves a more than comic effect. And did Cecil B. de Mille, the American Gance, really want to make a revue film when he shot his *Cleopatra* in 1934 (plate 175)?

Even in the early films about the Passion which are considered to be historically valid, like those made by Pathé, that fatal impression of 'oleography' is still there. In Cecil B. de Mille's first *Ten Commandments* (1922) there are grandiose sequences such as the pursuit of the

177 A neatly combed Moses quickly becomes kitsch. Cecil B. de Mille's *The Ten Commandments* of 1956.

Jews by the Egyptians and the crossing of the Red Sea, but in his second film (1956) there is an appreciable element of pomp and circumstance. One close-up of his neatly combed Moses with the tablets is intolerable (plate 177). The realistic details in almost all these biblical films becomes painful, even when directed by famous men such as John Huston, George Stevens or Nicholas Ray. The Hollywood tradition of Sunday-School sentimentality produced every incongruous cliché in the book.

211

Biblical characters can be interpreted only on either a heroic scale or on an unusually simple level. (The heroic element in Cecil B. de Mille's early films surrounds the characters in a sort of halo, in a

178 Hollywood traditions restrict a great director to oleography. Nicholas Ray's *King of Kings* (1960)

mysterious aura of myth.) Beyond these limits one inevitably falls into kitsch.

Pasolini's *The Gospel according to St Matthew* (1964) (plate 179) is convincing, thanks quite simply to its extreme simplicity; what we have here is timeless figures actually existing, not just actors playing them.

It is hard to draw any valid conclusion about a film one has not seen from a still taken out of context. It is clear that here one is up against imponderables that do not exist for the plastic arts.

179 A scene from Pasolini's *Gospel According to St Matthew*. This film by its studious simplicity avoids the danger of kitsch in treating a religious subject and reveals new possibilities.

In what are known as anticipation films, horror films or erotic films it is far easier to define the tendency towards kitsch. In Harry Hoyt's *Lost World* (1925) (plate 180) the papier mâché look of his prehistoric monsters is as grotesque as Roy del Ruth's crocodile-man (plate 181). When a director does not have the power of persuasion and the genius to impose the absurdity of another world on us as if it were real, kitsch is inevitable.

213

180 Papier mâché prehistoric monsters in Harry Hoyt's *Lost World* (1925).

181 Unexpectedly and grotesquely kitsch: Roy del Ruth's *Mammi Crocodilia* (1959)

182 Murnau has a genius which enables him to make a vampire acceptable: *Nosferatu* (1921–2).

In Freddie Francis's *The Skull* (1966) (plate 183), an English horror film, what are the elements that make it degenerate into painful kitsch? Perhaps the lascivious grimace of the young woman? And in Michel Garreras's *The Curse of the Mummy's Tomb* (1964) is it perhaps the exaggeratedly elegant behaviour of the girl with her arm in the grip of the mummy's hand as it tries to drag her away with it?

Horror, as Bela Balazs says with reference to Murnau's *Nosferatu* (1921-2) (plate 182), can stimulate our participation if we see it as an

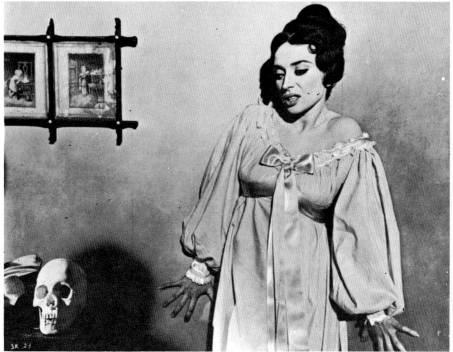

183 The combination of obscenity and horror produces kitsch. *The Skull* by Freddie Francis (1966)

icy wind blowing from another world and producing plausible images of reality.

What leads to deviations of taste, in both horror films and pseudo-erotic films, is the exploitation of the voyeurism and base instincts of the general public.

When Erich von Stroheim shows us a repellent cripple avidly gazing at the beautiful Mae Murray in *Merry Widow* (1925) or a similar scene in the rediscovered sequences of *Queen Kelly* (1928)

215

185 Pseudo-eroticism becomes pornokitsch in *Mondo di Notte no. 3*

with another cripple and the beautiful Gloria Swanson, what translates such scenes into great art is the corrosive shock effect of genius. If we look at a similar sequence in *Mondo di Notte* (1960) by Luigi Vanzi (plate 185) we find nothing but pornographic kitsch. In Stroheim's films, in which perversions are often raised to grandiose dimensions, disgust can become the measure of eroticism.

It is enough to compare such sequences by this great genius Stroheim – for example, the highly erotic emergence of the queen, white and naked, fresh and foaming from her bath, surrounded by guards – with the publicity photos of scantily clad stars, primarily those with Lily Damita or Joan Crawford, which were circulated by American agencies in the 'twenties and 'thirties, to realize that the latter have the same vulgar attraction as certain visiting cards handed out by expensive brothels.

Eroticism is as far removed from kitsch as the genuine terror one feels at the great (and very rare) horror films.

One can say, quite definitely, that kitsch in the cinema, as in all other art forms, is unpardonable mediocrity.

◄ 184 A publicity photo of the filmstar Lili Damita, circulated by American agencies in the 'twenties and 'thirties.

PORNOKITSCH AND MORALS

◄ 186 Jayne Mansfield's erotic appeal was never anything but kitsch.

Pornokitsch and morals *by Gillo Dorfles*

Even ethics have their kitsch, and here one should consider two fundamental facts:

1) that kitsch is essentially the falsification of sentiments and the substitution of spurious sentiments for real ones. That is to say that real feeling becomes sentimentality; this is the moral argument against kitsch.

2) that where ethics are in evidence the aesthetic component suffers.

One need only flick through the pages of pornographic magazines, visit dubious night clubs or look at the publicity photographs outside places like the Pigalle in Paris to find a mass of kitsch material. Perhaps this is a result of the moral degradation of our society? On the contrary, it is a form of aesthetic degradation due to the substitution of fictitious vice and pleasure for their authentic counterparts.

The rise of kitsch taste as an accessory to vice and pleasure began simultaneously with the appearance in the nineteenth century of the discreet brothel. Today a number of avant-garde-style cafés, prophets of 'good taste in bad taste', have reproduced the decorative style of these brothels in order to create a refined intellectual atmosphere on their premises. However, the vulgarity of this kind of decor was on the same level as the pleasure offered: it was a substitute for pleasure, legitimately dressed up. The legitimization of vice as pleasure added a further seal to the kitsch element.

Nevertheless it is possible to say that kitsch goes practically hand in hand with bourgeois morals, which are now in decline, although they reigned supreme in the golden age of kitsch in the first few decades of this century, cringing from the more open morals of the populace as well as from the decidedly corrupt morals in high places. It does not seem to me that great thieves, rakes or courtesans have ever been kitsch, but *petits bourgeois* with corrupted little minds certainly are.

◄ 187 In pornokitsch, sexual elements and elements of 'aesthetic' self-justification as well as others are mingled. The violin and 1900-style furniture are meant to create a refined and suggestive atmosphere.

Discourses on the nude in art are already obsolete, and discourses on nudo-kitsch, all the more so. To put it briefly, three quarters of the publications based on female (or male!) nudes which are flooding the West can be defined neither as being artistic nor as being anti-artistic. They are rather of sociological, psychological and pedagogic interest to us, but even this aspect interests us only marginally.

However, what does interest us is to see how often the display of photographic nudes of the straightforward erotic and commercial type is accompanied by a vast impedimenta of bad taste analogous to that of romantic comics and prurient literature.

Sophisticated or even sadistic pornography takes very diverse forms, and is often allied to avant-garde art forms – such as, for instance and in its day, Surrealism. In them the kitsch element, even when only just discernible as it is in the works of notable artists such as Delvaux, Magritte and Labisse, is exalted on aesthetic grounds so that anyone who questions the legitimacy of printing pornographic (or, as here, simply erotic) material is very smartly put in his place.

On the other hand, popular pornography in which the nude is shown for purely sexual and commercial reasons is one of the best vehicles of kitsch.

The suggestive poses and ambiguous smirks of the naked model or strip-tease artist are often characterized by a false modesty and condescending erotic implications. Their attitudes are heavily equivocal; suggestive without being positive, concealing and half revealing. The decorative apparatus which the nude uses consists of the worst kind of commonplaces. Creating a stale or strangely modernistic ensemble for example (plates 208-209 show a nude within a gilt frame). But what is more interesting is that the overall effect (and the girl herself) often looks rather abject, flabby and tired, showing how kitsch taste in 'beautiful anatomy' – and in this case kitsch anatomy – is the same as kitsch taste in art.

The fact that this pornography contains an unnatural element is borne out by the scant erotic or sexual appeal of the unembellished nude in its natural state. Evidently the lascivious element is supplied by features which in strictly moral terms could be called 'sinful', but which are in fact sinful in aesthetic terms rather than in moral terms and which reveal the presence of a *double-entendre* element with vicious undertones – this being another of the attributes of kitsch art.

'Pornokitsch' would probably deserve a broader coverage, especially today when this genre is becoming more widespread in many countries through the publication of photographic comics and artwork comics of erotic content. Even in this field a certain distinction must be drawn between genres: on the one hand there are comics like *Jodelle* which exploits its erotic element not only with some charm and a certain finesse in execution but also with evident self-irony; one should look too at that comic for the élite consisting of a graphic adaptation of *Zazie dans le Métro* by Queneau. On the other hand, there is the entirely different case of many cheap pornographic publications in which the erotic content is accompanied by the worst commonplaces of international bad taste.

This chapter on pornographic kitsch, the fruit of careful analysis, has been entrusted to Ugo Volli, a young student of sociology and philosophy.

Pornography and pornokitsch *by Ugo Volli*

The attempt to establish a link between kitsch and pornography, the introduction of a new aesthetic-ethical category and the neologism 'pornokitsch' itself – all these might at first appear if not exceptionable, at least questionable and not really justifiable.

In fact, although the time is past when concern with problems such as bad taste and pornography might seem a frivolous or purely modish occupation, the introduction of pornokitsch can raise at least two kinds of doubt.

It could be maintained that this is a superfluous pursuit because pornography is etymologically an inevitable example of bad taste (πόρνη meaning a prostitute of the lowest order) and thus there is no reason to distinguish pornokitsch from kitsch; or equally one could maintain that it is an unbecoming and erroneous pursuit because pornography is beyond any aesthetic considerations (though not beyond ethico-anthropological ones) and is purely for mindless consumption.

The airing of these two possible objections provides an opportunity to define and explain the meaning of pornokitsch and its distinction from pornography. The facts of sex have never been purely instinctual or physiological for man; they have always been pregnant with cultural, ritual, religious, aesthetic and sentimental significance[1]. Both pornography and pornokitsch are cultural and historical illustrations of man's attitude to sex. The first is a particular type of eroticism, slowly deformed by repression and morbidity; the second is false, sickly, sugary and slightly cold-blooded pornography adapted for kitsch-man.

Pornography is by nature crude and rough and raises no aesthetic or philosophical issues; it does not attempt to defend itself, does not try to hide its morbid character, and does not claim to be an art or a science[2].

Pornokitsch, however, besides being a negation of the genuinely human qualities of love and sex, is also the negation of pornography, whose crudeness, realism and, to a great extent, sexuality, it removes by means of the constant and systematic use of euphemistic techniques.

[1] The opposite theory is maintained by Desmond Morris in *The Naked Ape* (Cape, 1968) with fascinating though poorly demonstrated and scarcely scientific arguments. I would limit myself to appealing only to psycho-analytic theses (Freud, *Three Essays on Sexuality,* etc.) but this is an incontestable point.

[2] One need only think of de Sade's works, for example, for which only today some justification on aesthetic and philosophical grounds is being sought.

188 An illustration from a 'part publication' edition of Boccaccio's *Decameron*. Note the frieze surrounding the picture, meant to imitate ancient miniatures, in the presence of rather limited pornographic elements.

This is why pornography is an essentially non-aesthetic phenomenon for mindless consumption, and pornokitsch is a phenomenon involving the depravation of taste on an aesthetic as well as an anthropological level.

One obvious, though perhaps approximate way of confirming the fact that the two phenomena are distinct, lies in one characteristic which we have already mentioned: their historical continuity.

One can indicate with some precision if not the date of birth at least the historical factors which conditioned the origins and development of both pornography and pornokitsch.

Where pornography is concerned, in the sense in which we understand the term and have tried to define it above, we can only speak in

225

terms of those factors in the ancient world which arose from a certain type of religiosity which had always been latent in it but which triumphed in the Judaic-Christian tradition. On the one hand there was a predominantly emotional attitude towards sin – Kirkegaard called it fear, trembling and anxiety; on the other hand there was the extension of this attitude to cover everything corporeal and thus the world, man's flesh and the whole spectrum of sexual phenomena, understood as the origin and cosmic symbol of evil[3].

Pornography was the natural response to this sort of repression. It was the exaltation of the negativity of sex and its cheated fruition, because it was repressed and the subject of *angst*[4].

In contrast with this, pornokitsch was born simultaneously with kitsch-man and with his congenital inability either to take his sex raw or to be ashamed of it or to admit the existence of a radically negative component within himself: ethical romanticism[5], the bourgeois ideology of power, and neocapitalism were its natural premises. Out of his inability to live and see sex either authentically or as a sin, arose his need to justify it and to make it an aesthetic or scientific thing, either beautiful to behold or important to know, which would have no call on his personal responsibilities but would be looked upon with sentiment. In fact what arose from this jungle was the kitsch of Eros – pornokitsch.

It should be noted at this point that it is the subjective element, the way one uses it, that makes an erotic subject 'shameful' and thus pornographic, or lends it a facile and fatuous character, turning it into pornokitsch by means of a process of draining or substituting its significance, a process we might call decontextualization.

In this connection it should be remembered, as a prominent but not isolated example, that people in the West read works such as the *Kama Sutra* as if they were pornokitsch, and think of modes of thought such as tantra yoga, or yoga of sex, as pornokitsch, whereas these still have, even today, a real mystical and ritual value in their countries of origin, which is expressed in the sculptures of temples, themselves turned by us into pornokitsch[6].

[3] A comprehensive historical analysis justifying this attribution can be found in Wayland Young's *Eros Denied* (Weidenfeld and Nicolson, 1965, chapters VII, VIII, IX and *passim*). The material is extensive even if we cannot accept all its conclusions.

[4] On repression in general cf. Freud, *The hardship of civilization* and Marcuse, *Eros and civilization*.

[5] The expression is Croce's, from *Storia d'Europea nel secolo XIX* (Laterza, 1932).

[6] One should refer to the analysis of two Italian translations of Chinese texts, by C. Costa in *Sextrapolazioni,* an article which appeared in *Quindici*, no. 11, June 1968, in which the Italian translations of the *Disgrazie della Virtù* are also discussed.

Obviously, if we are treating the subjective aspects of these phenomena, we cannot forget that in order to feed the false and artificial sensibilities of kitsch-man, a culture industry has been set up, a wide and profitable (though often ignored) sector of which is involved in the diffusion of pornokitsch through the most varied media, from photography to literature, from drawings to the cinema and from advertising to strip-tease.

Even though one obviously cannot apply the selfsame comments to its use in each medium, it is probably possible to attempt one single analysis of the language of pornography and pornokitsch, inasmuch as its basic structure is used in various means of communication and therefore has a homogeneous core which is superimposed on whichever medium is used, though obviously modified to some extent for the particular purpose[7]. Thus the difference between a photograph, drawing or description of a pornokitsch subject is no greater than the difference between a literary text in printed, recorded or recitative form.

It is interesting to note how the culture industry, in its production of pornokitsch, or any other kitsch for that matter, uses mythagogic techniques to create new myths[8], facile yet carefully fabricated, which contrast not only with classic and popular mythology in the fact that they are entirely artificial, but also with the demystification of the scientific spirit, again through their falseness.

The link between myth and pornokitsch is particularly obvious – take for example the vamps, and women like Brigitte Bardot, Marilyn Monroe or Sophia Loren – but it is found in all pornokitsch, of which, as we shall see, it is an essential component.

The kinds of justification and euphemism[9] with which people seek to endow pornokitsch are many and varied and are adapted to the disguise given to the subject.

First of all there is something which we might call the kitsch of morals, a phenomenon which succeeds only in making sex an antiseptic and semi-scientific business, a 'thing' which should not be named, or a technical fact like reproduction in plants or star-fish.

[7] A structural analysis of pornographic language is certainly possible: See G. Dorfles, *Artificio e natura,* Einaudi, 1968, Chapter IX; U. Eco, *La struttura assente,* Bompiani 1968; R. Barthes, *Elements of symptomatology,* and the abundant literature on symptomatics and symptomatology. Perhaps one might take Propp's as a good model (V. Propp, *Morfologia della Fiaba,* Einaudi, 1966).

[8] G. Dorfles in *Nuovi Miti, Nuovi Riti* (Einaudi) and R. Barthes in *Miti d' Oggi* have written on contemporary mythology and the reasons for its artificiality as well as its component parts.

[9] Euphemisms, along with myths, are essential components of pornokitsch, in so far as we can use one to find the other and *vice versa.* For a general review of this see N. Galli De' Paratesi, *Semantica dell' eufemismo.*

227

Sex education films like *Helga* or *Eva* (plate 189) proudly claim that they are recommended by medical, academic and religious authorities; there are magazines which claim that they show photographs of female nudes for the purposes of sexual education and moral and psychological health (the slogan of a French magazine of this type was, until a short time ago, *Plexus décomplexe*); there are books which claim to be able to show anyone the way to sexual ecstasy and harmony – all claim the highest human and moral motives, as their detractors also do.

The man who sells pornography does so not for his own profit but in order to fulfil an important mission; the man who buys it does so not for his own pleasure but to educate and civilize himself; the man who is opposed to it is not really disturbed or upset by it, but is trying to safeguard the most sacred values of Western civilization.

Already one can see how pornokitsch is different from pornography in the fact that it is designed for the most hypocritical mentality, the *'bel esprit'* of the bourgeoisie that buys it. Kitsch-man cannot admit that his use of erotic material is a form of voyeurism, a morbid act

189 The fashion for 'sexual education' films has more or less supplanted 'sexy' films. None of the attractions of this film is omitted from the blurb: from the breaking of an *ancient silence*, a *tabu*, to the fact that *the film contains scenes which for their realism might be considered unsuitable for the younger viewer* despite *being for everyone;* to the presence of a *nurse* in case *any members of the public faint during the child-birth scene.* The film claims to be educational, and thus approved by medical and, of course, religious authorities, though it is still inflammatory and possibly dangerous.

190 Advertisements for beauty products and underwear are often based on pornokitsch elements, and are meant to provoke the sexual inferiority complexes latent in the average reader.

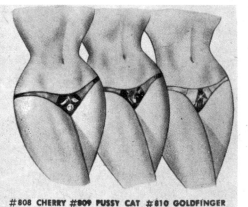
involving his entire personality; he prefers to believe that it is some-thing from which he remains detached, a sort of technical instruction or education, as we have seen, or else something for aesthetic con-templation.

To this euphemistic aspect of pornokitsch, namely the one we have called the moral aspect, is added another form of justification which is much more complex and long-winded. This we might call the aes-thetic justification.

All the aspects of pornographic communication and the full potential of the various media are used to give pornokitsch an easily acceptable aesthetic appeal, banal and debased, this characteristic being common to all forms of kitsch.

229

191 This photograph, according to the magazine that published it, is *a new interpretation of the original sin.* As an example of pornokitsch exoticism it is worthy of note.

192 *Right* The *double-entendre* of this photograph accompanied an invitation to subscribe to the magazine in which it was published. The phallic symbolism of the bird, emphasized by its long beak, makes this picture a classic of its kind.

In the first place an artificially avant-garde style of writing is used, so as to delude the reader by presenting him with the prospect of enjoying 'art prose' or 'artistic nudes' photographed or painted, and in doing so trying to elevate kitsch as high as possible through the means of communication selected. Thus the written language is loaded with adjectives, 'poetic' images, rhetorical figures of speech and metaphors piled one on top of the other without any logical or aesthetic links. Hyperbole, metaphor abound. The aim is to stun and intoxicate the reader, to give him the impression, by means of a facile neglect of syntax, that he is confronted with 'art prose'. But the aim is also to excite him surreptitiously by letting slip sexual symbols which are perfectly obvious, though concealed by the torrent of prose.

In an attempt to construct a new myth on every page and to find

new magic characteristics for every woman, even classical images, noble words and erudite references of a uniquely scholastic culture are not sacred: the woman becomes a *nymph from the woods* or a *goddess,* often *Venus* or a *Greek statue,* sometimes a *fairy* or a *sprite.* She is immersed in mythology and exists in the most exotic latitudes.

In reality, all this tinsel and glitter has a specific function – to exalt the sexual basis of pornokitsch, while at the same time to veil it by enveloping it in atmospheres and situations made as unreal and fabulous as possible.

Very often this process of veiling and concealment involves the substitution of terms such as 'fantasy', 'dream', 'imagination', 'fairy-tale' and so on for the fabulous descriptions. These function as key words for the subject, who reacts to them as if they were Pavlovian stimuli, in a predetermined way and exactly as he is meant to. These key words are very great in number because they have the same effect as the classicizing descriptions of woman which we mentioned above, namely to substitute for the description a semantic halo of suggestive words or phrases producing an effect of ambiguity which, rather than being poetic, is banal and debased.

This kind of phenomenon can be found above all in the captions and commentaries to the photographs of the pornographic magazines, in which literary pornokitsch achieves its most striking manifestations.

In such writings the atmosphere of ambiguity of which we have spoken is completely useless, firstly because the content of the picture is described and the reader has seen it for himself, and secondly because he becomes acclimatized to unreality, dream and fantasy as invoked by the customary use of connotations and rhetorical prose figures.

An example of this sort of writing, itself not among the most involved or complex conceptually and linguistically, is given below. It consists of part of the text which originally accompanied plate 193:

Altogether, even though we may be losing patience and fighting against thin air, and there are all the little pieces that we have not succeeded in putting in their right place, there is still the fact of this beautiful blonde girl with her dress out of 1001 Nights. And perhaps Mimmo Lisa [the model's name, which we know already] is neither Swedish nor Sicilian. She emerged with her empire-style topless in the form of a puff of azure smoke from a bottle or an amphora, to which she will run to hide at the stroke of midnight like a Cinderella.

The facts which emerge from this fragment of caption (and indeed from the entire text and any of its kind: the example is quite random) are very scant. We have the name of the model, which anyone who has read the rest already knew and which in any case is of minimal importance; her physical characteristics, which are apparent in the photograph along with her comic costume and which get the same pompous treatment in the text. There remains the entirely artificial problem of her origins, which certainly doesn't make the publishers 'lose patience', because they know it; and the reader couldn't care less. She might look Swedish (and therefore exotic – a superficial and ingenuous but significant example of the sexual racism that is characterized by the term 'Latin lover') and Sicilian . . . because of her name.

Thus we have all the features – the dreamlike atmosphere, the dissolution of reality into dream, and the mythical side, in which the

232

193 Mimmo Lisa, whose 'history' is told in the text.

reference to two different myths is interesting as well as being incongruous – the *genies* of the *Thousand and One Nights* and the
Germanic *fairies:* and Cinderella somehow tacked on to the other
two.

   The two other media are subjected to analogous processes, that is
to a facile and banal use of aesthetic features worn so thin as to have
lost any effect, and to the not always implicit claim that these features
are 'artistic' and therefore 'justify' the content.

Where photography is concerned the work of the men who call themselves, with a good measure of boastful ingenuity, *the masters of
beauty* is particularly interesting. They photograph nearly always in
black and white and have an unusual talent for photographs superimposed, subimposed and soft-focussed, with varying textures, distorted perspectives and unusual light effects including attempts at

233

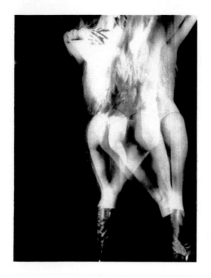

194–95 Stroboscopic effects and other photographic paraphernalia seldom help to achieve aesthetic effect. These photographs constitute an attempt to lay a veneer of modernity and sophistication over the usual female nude.

stroboscopic effects (plates 194–5). It is almost superfluous to say that, despite the display of technique, the pictures all look much the same, without any particular novelty or aesthetic interest apart from a certain pretextual and languid pleasingness and an obvious desire to present the picture as 'beautiful' or 'artistic'.

196–97 The same pose, drawn and photographed, can assume profoundly different values on the aesthetic level.

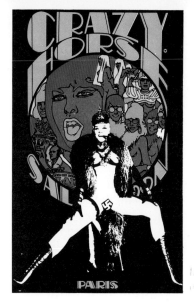

198–99 'The political element', in the form of a swastika, is intended to justify this picture to an easily satisfied public.

This rhetorical apparatus, too, like its literary parallel, evidently offers some sort of justification to the reader and producer of the material in that, being 'artistic', it cannot be pornographic.

These then are the real producers of pornokitsch, who insist on the existence of a distinction between their work and pornography, analogous to the one we have explained but obviously quite different in substance.

Looking at it another way, one of the most common arguments used in the justification of pornokitsch asserts that the human body, and the female body in particular, is 'the most beautiful thing in the world'. This assertion contains both the identification of kitsch beauty and pleasingness and the concept, or rather the myth of the *woman object,* which is a part of the bourgeois syndrome of the rejection of the idea of flesh and which lies at the root of all pornokitsch, or at least that designed for men.

The same things might well be said of pornographic drawing, which often turns out to be kitsch. This is certainly admissible in theory, and sometimes it happens that pornographic elements are used in serious drawing (but can this be called pornography? The answer to this is no, on the basis of the considerations explained above. It has even less right to be called pornokitsch, except when it is a case of *ostranenie* (or estrangement) or indeed of the classic use of kitsch elements in a context which estranges them from their usual environment, making an element of some serious value out of them)[10].

[10] On the concept of *ostranenie* (estrangement) (which is completely different from the *decontextualization* which we have mentioned above) see G. Dorfles, *Artificio e natura,* pp. 234-6 and V. Erlich, *Il formalismo russo* (Bompiani, 1966).

Much more often, however, it is pornographic drawing that seeks to adapt itself to current styles and to draw some justification from them; and, given that there is decidedly little room for the human figure in modern painting, other than in socialist realism, some examples of pictorial kitsch, or more simply in some pictures by those who refuse to accept new trends, as well as in pop painting, whose amplified comics are, however, not so easy to reconcile with kitsch – given all this, draughtsmen whose talents lie in the depiction of the human figure are forced to draw women's fashions, comics and furnishing styles. Thus they lose all contact with the real world by employing modes of expression which are truly artistic but have been overtaken by time.

Thus, like Art Nouveau itself, pornokitsch contains certain neo-Art Nouveau characteristics, along with neo-Gothic, pseudo- surrealist or naive works. Here, too, symbols are scattered everywhere, allusions are rife and the image is heavily detailed to give 'artistic' value and, surreptitiously, to accentuate the sexuality of the figure.

But the side of pornokitsch that we have called aesthetic covers more than the use of a false artisticity and a pseudo-modern prose style; besides this some importance is attached to the euphemization of the pornographic subject. Here too the techniques employed are diverse, with a multiplicity of variations, but all can be used in an attempt to hide the pornographic reality by means of any argument that seems autonomous and relevant, and possibly cultural or 'artistic' as well, though in reality no more than a pretext.

This gives rise to biographies and 'romanticized' histories of a specific kind (for example those of Lucretia Borgia or Catherine of Russia); it gives rise also to the books which depict 'ethnologically' or 'historically' the sexual habits of 'exotic' foreign peoples (including even Parisians as exotic) or of ancient civilizations, with reconstructions on whose accuracy and fidelity any comment would be superfluous; and 'realistic' literary products, obviously entirely without value.

It is also particularly interesting that works which once were properly pornographic and devoid of kitsch associations are now read as pornokitsch. Boccaccio, de Sade, Catullus, Sappho, Ovid and Flaubert have all suffered this sad fate.

This type of reading, which is analogous to what we mentioned above, though slightly different from it—the reading of works which were not originally pornographic—has provoked the publication of a great mass of new editions of certain types of classic, heavily modified and cut, with illustrations and sometimes photographs, summaries

236

and sometimes translations. In the latter connection one awful example was a translation of Boccaccio's *Decameron* into modern Italian, illustrated with fake miniatures and absurd photographs, the whole being blatantly pornokitsch, and, to make matters worse, published in weekly instalments. As one can imagine, the result was obscene in every sense of the word.

200 Nature is an element often used in pornokitsch to create an effect of 'spontaneity' and 'purity', both of which the *medium* has already definitively destroyed.

Nor is it safe to assume that the figurative arts of the past have been exempt from this sort of treatment with its attendant dangerous and serious effects. This form of kitsch is quite common in pornographic photographs, and its manifestations in them are extremely complex: here we have exoticism justifying (under the guise of geographic or tourist interest) photographs of beautiful and less beautiful girls,

237

nude or semi-nude and playing Indians, Chinese, Vietnamese, Negresses and Hawaiians (plate 201): or we have history justifying the most pathetic reconstructions of, for instance, Marie Antoinette in various poses and her underwear, the 'Pharaohs' (plate 202), Greek statues, Pompeian frescoes, Goyas and Titians; all terrible to behold. In classical art the editors of pornographic magazines and their eternally resourceful photographers have discovered a new art, which consists of painting a model with dots and circles or psychedelic

201 Pseudo-naturalism and exoticism are both found in this picture, called *Luana, the daughter of the virgin forest,* providing an evident stimulus for kitsch-man's desire to escape.

lines and strokes (plate 204), presenting the whole as a work of the greatest aesthetic interest.

Another way to use art or its name is that which involves 'fixing in colour the glory of the woman-symbol of the 'sixties', in this case Ursula Andress, painted in a vaguely classical pose and with a background of similar tone, the technique displaying slightly spurious classical connotations, and the sum effect, aided by the massive gilt frame, being distinctly comic (plate 205).

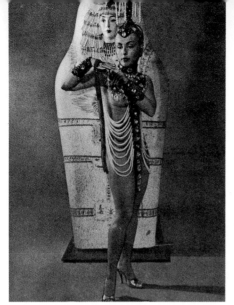

202–203 The sarcophagus behind the female Pharaoh and the statues enclosing Lisa Gastoni are both used to justify the photographs by means of their reference to romantic antiquity.

204 A model to be painted is a recurrent feature in pornokitsch magazines. Often the caption explains that 'in the life-class anyone can paint'.

Sometimes, by way of an alternative, it is the artist who allows himself to be used, and so we have the inevitable Dali arranging a furiously pornokitsch room for a model in a body stocking, without any qualms about appearing in the picture himself (plate 206). For further examples of pornokitsch we can look to the model framing her

n: 'Time, inevitably, kills
la Andress, for example.
t to think about it. So a
of the woman-symbol of the
k for itself when summer has

ited by Dali in a late   ▶
h retains only the most banal

breasts in a gilt frame (plates 208-9), the comic recounting the life and loves of Cagliostro, which illustrates in a childish but unequivocal way the beauty of his innumerable women, or the sexy photoromances, among which perhaps the most interesting are the science-fiction ones. In these, shipwrecked cosmic mariners or explorers from the future rush around making love (sometimes they have to make love to survive) on our earth and in our age, transforming the bodies of their partners and their own bodies with more lust than indifference and uttering incomprehensible sounds in their own language during their orgasms.

But the maximum level of pornokitsch content is reached by a series which appeared in Italian and French magazines 'for men', entitled 'living Rodin'. Evidently Rodin did not intend his sculptures to be alive, but here they are interpreted in a series of photographs in which males and females, quite naked, assume the poses of some of Rodin's famous statues, giving an obviously false interpretation which fails to respect even the fundamental aesthetic qualities of the original (plates 210-11).

All these instances have a prominent kitsch significance; here too the bourgeois, the *bel esprit,* the kitsch-man can enjoy his pornography with a tranquil, complex-free mind, for the subject has a declared 'artistic' and cultural content, not because the medium makes use of any aesthetic forms, as we have seen above, but because the artistic reference is quite direct. This much-stressed connotation constantly reassures the reader of the seriousness of the work and is continuously re-iterated in captions and commentaries.

Here, as in the rest of the kitsch of this medium, the model does not exist as a person, nor even as the embodiment of the intoxicating eroticism that is the essence of true and proper pornography. She is simply a vehicle of 'aesthetic' or 'cultural' values which estrange her from us.

This, among others, is the reason why we have called pornokitsch the negation of pornography. The models in 'living Rodin', for example, lose not only any individuality and any authentically erotic qualities; by assuming a certain type of pose they immediately stop being a sexual subject: this is what the producers of the pornographic magazines claim when they assert that they are not producing pornography – and indeed they are not. The model is not an object of sexual desire, but an interesting aesthetic fact (either in herself or by means

◀ 207 Even debased science fiction is used as a pretext to illustrate intercourse between beautiful humans and horrific space monsters.

Galleria d'arte

Niente da dire.
Se il nudo
non è osceno,
e finalmente non lo è
anche sulla scorta
del tribunali,
il nudo nel riquadro
di una cornice
è persino qualcosa
di meglio: è arte.
Così, ammirando
questa ragazza
dalla bellezza classica,
non ci sembra
nemmeno di sfogliare
una rivista, ma ci pare
quasi di passeggiare,
assorti, per la Galleria
Borghese.

208–209 In this *art gallery, the nude is art;* and as the magazine says, 'when admiring this girl with her classical beauty one no longer seems to be flicking through the pages of a magazine, but strolling absorbed through the Borghese Gallery'.

of the medium) or else she presents an interesting historical or ethnographical document, and so on.

However, even at this point the pornokitsch process is not finished, for probably, at least on a subconscious level, and often on a conscious level the tinsel falls, the glitter fades, and it is revealed as an excuse, a sad apology for the real thing – and pornokitsch is looked at with new eyes, as pure and proper pornography. The female model in 'living Rodin', in fact, is not appreciated as a 'statue' or 'an attempt at a statue' or even as a 'girl trying to pass herself off as a statue'; no, she is revealed as a desirable woman because of her physical attractions, though only in a false, morbid and depersonalized way, as in all pornography. But she is at least seen in a more human, sincere and natural light than she had initially been.

244

To this cycle of autonegation, euphemism and mystification one can add yet another form of pornokitsch, possibly the most clumsy, banal and primitive: this is found almost solely firstly in photographs which combine and juxtapose pornography and kitsch objects, and secondly in those which depict falsely simple and natural situations intended to justify the pornography.

210–211 The most blatant example of 'artistic' pornokitsch is 'Living Rodin'. The difference in effect between the original statue and the pose of the models is clearly visible. Apart from the effect conferred by the *medium*, the difference in attitudes shows how different the effects desired are despite the superficial similarity.

In the first case, for example, the models are unexpectedly involved with statues and armour, or with more explicit symbols like snakes and weapons (plate 212). In the second category they might be walking nude in leafy woods or playing in the ever azure waters of lakes and waterfalls, frolicking in ordinary rooms, or anywhere from mountain-huts where they pose clad in magnificent bearskins, to drawing-rooms or bedrooms, which might perhaps offer some justification for their nudity.

The invention is to construct a story round every picture and to adhere to a constant pattern of myth, enabling the reader to enter into the world of the photograph and in some way make it his own. One particular case is that of pornokitsch in advertising, in which the equivocality between the concealment and exhibition of sexuality, which we have already examined, is complicated by a further euphemistic issue; in fact the presence of sexual stimulus in the product advertised must be clear to be effective. But in order that the prospective buyer's feelings of 'independence' and 'autonomy' should not be offended, he should not be made to notice this stimulus positively, especially if the relationship between the stimulus and the product is artificial.

Another careful distinction must also be made in such cases. For example the sexy aspect in advertisements for drinks or cars can be much more heavily loaded with pornokitsch elements than advertisements for bras or perfumes.

There is also a traditional pornokitsch which was in vogue in the golden years of the beginning of this century but which has now lost all its force and emotional impact. This manifested itself in the form of objects shaped as women, or parts of the female body. The shapes of the women's bodies are now grossly dated, but these pieces often took the form of exotic china figurines depicting coloured women, executed with evident ingenuity. All of them, now abandoned and obsolete, border on the comic and ridiculous even in the eyes of those who take the pornographic magazines of today seriously. But it should not be forgotten that with all the changes in taste the function of these objects has remained the same and the removal of the myth which surrounded them, which time alone has wrought, is a process which the pornokitsch of today will soon undergo, too.

Up till now we have examined the principal stages through which eroticism has been debased to pornography, and pornography to pornokitsch; we have found that it is largely a process of successive negations and extractions of meaning, of decontextualization, as we have called it.

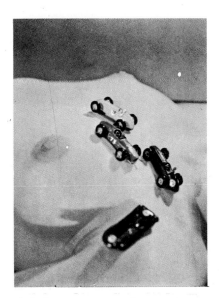

212 The use of more or less obvious phallic symbols is very common in pornokitsch photographs. This picture is part of a series in which the model, carressed by the snake, at first assumes an expression of horror but gradually begins to show ever increasing pleasure.

213 By means of a process of alienation and decontextualisation which exploits an inversion of pornokitsch priorities, it is possible to heighten the interest of a picture such as this one.

214–215 Eroticism and horror are often wed in kitsch.

216–218 The trash of traditional kitsch, with its *double-entendres* and heavy ambiguities is now obsolete and survives only as the taste of those educated at the beginning of the century.

The woman becomes an object, the vehicle of a set of values not her own and in any case faked and intended to mislead. Her sex loses all human meaning and in a way she retreats within herself to hide herself and makes herself invisible; everything becomes misty and confused, submerged in a great mass of spurious mystique.

One might well ask oneself what happens when the pornokitsch process is taken to the very limit, and what the sum effect of the anti-sexuality of pornokitsch is when taken to the point where it becomes a negation of itself. This is the case in some photographs in which the female body appears as a purely formal element, deprived not only of all aesthetic and sexual associations but also of its representational capacity. The breasts of the model, for example, become the weights on a balance which a little man drawn on the stomach is trying to lift. She herself, on the other hand, is represented by the 'master of beauty' using distorted perspectives; or else her body becomes a race-course for cars (plate 213).

219 A typical card of the beginning of the century

Here we are confronted with the comic [11], that is with a form of estrangement fairly analogous to that of the assimilation of kitsch elements by valid works; however, one cannot say that the aesthetic results achieved in this way, even when not counterfeit, are noteworthy or even valid.

Certainly, however, one can state that the exaggeration of the structure of pictures of this kind provides a way to escape from pornokitsch, as an anthropological fact, again, rather than an aesthetic one.

With this problematic possibility of redemption one might conclude this study of pornokitsch as the product of the culture industry.

It would be expedient at this stage to give the term its fullest breadth of meaning in order to be able to gather into it all kitsch-man's attitudes to sex and love.

If it is indeed true that pornokitsch draws its origins from kitsch-man's use of pornography and his subsequent industrialization of the fruits of his use of pornography, then one must also take into consideration the existence of pornokitsch on a subjective personal level, which precedes objective and industrialized kitsch. Kitsch-man's love, sex-life, complexes and feelings are not only the real origins, but also the real expression, of pornokitsch. They are the factors which determine and explain the phenomena which we have described. These phenomena are not substantially different from other examples of broader pornokitsch such as popular romances or the words of pop songs[12].

In this study it is not possible to demonstrate the unity that we have postulated, but one need only look at the studies already compiled on the matters we have discussed to convince oneself that these phenomena present a tightly united front. They constitute one of the most remarkable depravations of Western society, and can only be definitely wiped out by a profound revolution, a socialist one, at its roots.

---

[11] For the interpretation of the comic as the estrangement and mechanization of man see G. Dorfles, *Artificio e natura,* Chap. IV. The comic in pornography might be compared with the comic in the film, both being the exaggeration of an anti-naturalistic mechanicality in the reproduction of the human figure. One should also bear in mind Freud's phrase on the characteristic inherent in the comic of sublimating the libido.

[12] See Stranieri *et al., Le canzoni della cattiva coscienza* (Bompiani).

STYLING AND ARCHITECTURE

Styling and architecture *by Gillo Dorfles*

Kitsch is as common in what is new as it is in what is old, which is a natural state of affairs. Once we have established that the arrival of kitsch – or at least its most exuberant aspect – coincides with the arrival of the automobile, we can only expect mechanized production to nurture kitsch elements as much as, if not more than, any other elements.

The rapid spread of modern furniture (steel-tubed and Danish-type) and electrical household appliances (refrigerators, American kitchens, TV sets etc.) provided immediate inspiration for elements in this area as well.

The advantage, yet at the same time the disadvantage, is that the difference between the authentic model and its imitated version is not that well-defined. This was the case, for example, when an Italian firm bought the patent of the famous steel-tubed chair-cum-armchair designed by Marcel Breuer, and put it on the market twenty years after its initial launching. Had it not been for the respect people bore the inventor, it would have been said quite confidently that this was basically kitsch furniture, an imitation of superseded modern furniture.

In fact the normal process of obsolescence is often enough to make such manufactured products out-moded and vaguely kitsch. The huge radiograms of several years ago which were the *dernier cri* of fashion today appear technically interesting but definitely kitsch where taste is concerned. As for the phenomenon of the revival of old motor-cars, the fact that one enthuses over their elegance and line can almost always be attributed to fashion, to the fact that it is expensive to restore these cars, and that their slightly grotesque and ingenuous appearance adds a certain fascination to the often mediocre bodywork, which has undeniably been superseded both technically and aesthetically speaking.

There is, however, another aspect, still involving motor-cars, where one can more easily make a clear distinction between models in good and bad taste: this is the use of excessive styling, especially where American coachwork is concerned. Styling naturally affects any

◄ 220 The survival of kitsch involves a special private and domestic dimension where objects and furniture, which have no particular characteristics, *per se*, exist in an atmosphere of mediocre and fanciful 'arrangements'.

253

industrial product and is in evidence when an article is re-designed for greater decorative and showy effect purely and simply for sales reasons – in other words, when the object is submitted to a particular 'cosmetic' treatment which accentuates the line, and the so-called aerodynamic quality, but has no basic and genuine functional purpose. The American car, which is particularly overloaded with gaudy details, chromium and electrical gadgets, is thus the fulfilment of a typical kitsch phenomenon.. But where in this case does the kitsch phenomenon begin and end? This is hard to define, because even the die-hard advocates of absolute functionalism have had to recognize that there is always an aesthetic *as well as* a utilitarian factor in industrial design; and when shall we be able honestly to say that a mass-produced article designed to satisfy the demands of the public at large does not contain kitsch elements?

The form most affected by this question of styling in design is architecture, which, perhaps more than any other contemporary art, incorporates a purely functional *and* a prevalently artistic aspect, and can contain the greatest discrepancies between the two.

If in the past this art more than any other had a function that expressed a given culture through the monumental, religious and political edifices it produced, it is today, with the arrival of new construction materials the intervention of new techniques, and (in a different way) the decline of religious and political monumental art, destined more often than not to perform a purely utilitarian function or to garnish this function with tinsel and unnecessary excrescences which remove it from rather than unite it with the trends of contemporary art, and affiliate it instead to kitsch. For this reason architectural kitsch can take on two fundamental aspects: the aspect of a summary and a *rifacimento* of past styles – as is the case with various revivals of the last century – or that of an eavesdropped *rifacimento* and an imitation of recent styles (the phoney Corbusier, the phoney Wright, the phoney Aalto): both these aspects are inevitable and merit being cited as examples of kitsch.

No-one in our opinion is better qualified than Vittorio Gregotti to present a full discussion of architectural kitsch and contemporary design, which is why we have asked him to tackle this delicate task.

Kitsch and architecture *by Vittorio Gregotti*

During the last ten years at least, a new attitude in architecture and design towards the question of kitsch can clearly be recognized. It is an attitude which has not as yet resulted in any practical outcome, and has still to define its own terms of reference and produce concrete examples; it is more easily discernible in critical writings and academic research, and occasionally in speculative Utopian schemes, but in spite of all this the presence of kitsch can nevertheless be detected. The traces are already as easily to be found in the context of the urban scene, the great cities or large-scale infrastructures, as in the concentrated centres of distribution or the highly organized industrial complexes. In all these instances the prevailing conditions produce a state of such overcrowding and such insensitivity that individual buildings and objects often lose their significance or even their own identity. This fact only highlights the need both for an urgent reappraisal of the use of architectural materials and for the increasing adoption of more highly complex and less narrowly defined determining factors with the metaphysical implications involved in their handling and treatment. In recent years these factors have presented new problems both with regard to the creative impulse behind the production of individual objects or works of architecture, and also with regard to their availability and use.

As a result of these new attitudes the demarcation line which separated kitsch and the avant-garde about thirty years ago now appears broken and ill-defined. Architects have a fresh outlook (and it would appear that the same phenomenon holds true in general for all creative art), and are willing to re-assess the nature of kitsch and to consider it once again in cultural terms. They are prepared to entertain its possible use, not in a spirit of irony or antagonism, but with a real enthusiasm which might well lead them to discover, in that same rather vague sphere to which the whole tradition of the modern movement was once opposed, new and more comprehensive methods of controlling the processes which shape our material environment.

It is of course possible that this change is also the result of an urge for self-abnegation, and evidence of an intellectual rejection of the planning process, when this process is equated with repression, or what is worse is regarded as a weapon in the hands of hostile influences. Nevertheless, the phenomenon has an innate consistency, even in the sphere of architecture, which on a critical level enhances and crystallizes our ideas of the nature of kitsch.

What then are the basic causes of this phenomenon? Why is it always revolutionary? What is its essential nature?

In the first place it can be said that this change is connected with the recent development of a highly urbanized environment, the technological processes of mass-production, and the widespread growth of communications systems. Secondly, current cultural trends regard kitsch as a form of exorcism of the world of industry and mass-consumption; we feel a wave of sympathy for those products which, by their philistine quality, demonstrate at one and the same time the blindness of industrial production and the assumed indispensability of the intellectual; the adoption of a kitsch attitude gives us the opportunity of disguising and dismissing the usefulness of the objects which we are offered.

221 The density and stratification of the urban scene are two of the generative components of architectonic kitsch.

222 Remedies put forward to cure the urban crisis often create 'pretty and restful landscapes', which however are crammed with small kitsch elements.

Finally, there is a very real hope of completing the historical cycle of the kitsch object, as we have understood it up to now, through the growth of mass-culture and a manifesto which restates in fresh terms questions of taste and the traditional relationships between producers and consumers, quantity and quality, major and minor cultures, style and method. A new set of symbols and values emerges, in contrast to the old conception of the contemplative enjoyment of a work of art, which shaped kitsch-man.

The tendency is towards a grasp of the many ways in which an object can be handled and used, towards a lively understanding of the way in which it communicates and the substance of what it has to communicate, towards a clarification of the relationship between ends and means, and finally towards unbiased means of expression.

This interplay between kitsch and mass-culture, with its various subtle relationships has been well described by Umberto Eco in the chapter of his book *Apocalittici ed Integrati* devoted to the analysis of bad taste. The fact is that we still find ourselves acting simultaneously on various levels, for there is no clear distinction between an emergent mass-culture and a culture of the élite which watches its birth-pangs with growing interest, and they are themselves both submerged in a vast belt of midcult which coincides completely with the traditional conception of kitsch. The result is clearly to be seen in the field of architecture, especially if we use the term architecture

223 Two plastic trees planted in marble certainly confer prestige and 'elegance' to the window of this porter's lodge in a New York block. The effect is not unpleasing in spite of the various components of the 'laws of kitsch'.

to cover the planning and execution on every level of the total physical environment in which we live. Nowadays such an environment will already have undergone a process of concretion, and will have involved the increasingly rapid transformation of nature to a cultural realization in material terms. Nature has been exploited technologically and has become artificial, and though its diminution is more conducive to social survival, it is only at the expense of burdening it with a conglomeration of artefacts. The end result is that our present-day world is so cluttered that any attempt at environmental planning involves not only the ordering of nature but the resolution of the meaning and reason behind man's achievements, this new profusion of objects which first and foremost impose upon their surroundings their own atmosphere, progression, style and advancement. We are faced with a confused but exuberant vitality which lets loose upon the world a flood of goods whose quantity is not necessarily matched by their quality. The concrete form which our new surroundings take comprehends a multiplicity of objects, unrelated in scale and as often as not linked only by the actual process of accretion. The environment grows, sprawls, dissipates itself and leaves behind it a trail of refuse, all as a concomitant of our activi-

224 An invitation to kitsch

ties. Its relationship with us becomes ever more imperious as it virtually imposes upon us the laws of a second nature whose characteristics, whether on an urban or a domestic scale, whether in the house, in the city or in the country, stem in the great majority of cases from the conception of kitsch as a midcult.

Modern man, and by this is meant the average petit-bourgeois who is the product of our technological culture, now enjoys the pleasures of nature on a kitsch level, either through the exploitation of the landscape for tourism or by carving the Rocky Mountains into more authentic examples of the contemporary scene, as if they were in the same category as an ancient monument or even examples of modern architecture itself. The true work of art suffers expulsion into the literal isolation of the museum, or is set behind the railings of those little enclosures which fence off and offer a spurious protection to ancient monuments, whose attributes are reduced to their archeological significance and their tourist interest. Hence, though lip service may be paid to their importance, they become in fact detached from the operation of the historical process and are captured, dissected, assimilated, diffused and consumed to suit the purposes of kitsch-man's utilization of artistic works.

This process has brought about that large-scale degeneration of our environment which transcends rather than ignores the problems of function and is essentially motivated towards the kitsch ideal – the debasement of real character to a form of bogus folklore.

As we have already said, this decline is the end result of a lack of planning and the absence of a judicious balance between ends and means, where planning is defined as embracing not only the practical predisposition of means and resources but also the use of the critical

225 Modern man, usually the middle-class product of technological culture, has reduced to the level of kitsch the enjoyment of his environment and the products of man's highest achievements, such as these copies of art masterpieces from the Louvre in the Paris metro station of the same name.

faculty to ensure the integrity of the finished product, that negative aspect of thought which is present in every valid project which sets out to dissociate itself from what already exists or has been used before, and aspires to fresh levels of conception.

It is true that today we are in a position to recognize fully the close tie between forward-planning and conservation, but we have also shown that large-scale distribution could in itself militate against kitsch, and that kitsch does not simply represent the debasement of an élite culture faced with the inexorable need for mass-distribution, but has its own well-defined ideology and its own characteristic structure. The kitsch object, within the limits of its structural framework, acts in a degree as a catalyst with regard to reality and in so doing allows genuinely creative works to achieve a new relationship with that selfsame reality and at the same time a fresh perception of the world. Yet this is but a caricature of the catalytic process or rather a transference from the principles involved to the end result. A glass becomes 'new and original' in kitsch terms if its size for example is inflated out of all proportion to its function, although that function can still be fulfilled, unlike pop art where impracticability is a *sine qua non*. The transformation is achieved by a change of material or the use of inappropriate materials, the disguising of the object's function or by the contrast between the form which it often assumes of a different but easily recognized object and its own essential form: a cigarette lighter in the shape of a sailing-boat or a lipstick, and a lipstick masquerading as the Leaning Tower of Pisa. Lastly, there sometimes takes place a fundamental break in which the planning principles underlying the basic structure of an object or piece of architecture or an environment are used with a studied disregard for the ideological background which alone gives them their true significance. This happened, for example, in the case of the modern movement and its association with the concepts of rationalization and functionalism. The movement was conceived as

226 A glass becomes 'new and original' in the kitsch operation, if its dimensions, for example, are magnified beyond the scale of its function.

261

a radical reformation in which a whole social class became aware of its political responsibilities and governed on a strictly rational basis. Its basic principle that form is dependent on function set out to rediscover the interrelated elements which make up the essential structure of an architectonic system, by an impartial analysis of the problems inherent in the system itself. Kitsch culture merely makes use of the same method to cheapen the means of production. The principle of functionalism is reduced to the lowering of costs and the raising of profit margins; 'the basic minimum', the ideological principle behind the ordinary commercial firm, has simply become a

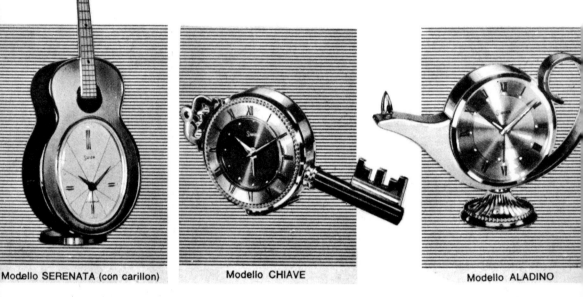

Modello SERENATA (con carillon)   Modello CHIAVE   Modello ALADINO

227 Transference of meaning is achieved in this instance by absurd contrast between the shape of the clock and the shape of some other clearly identifiable object.

method of maximizing the use of the firm's resources. Frank Lloyd Wright held that 'the nature of the materials dictates the speed of the construction'; Adolf Loos asserted that 'ornament is tantamount to crime'; and both dicta are invoked as a means of reducing labour costs. What started as an ethical principle has degenerated into a means of exploitation, and creative discovery now descends to kitsch.

262

Yet we may still ask how much of midcult was already inherent in those same idealistic principles of modern culture, or to what extent the concern for humanity, the focus on the housing problem and the family unit and that same preoccupation with the potential broadening of the benefits of art are also embodied in the principles of kitsch and serve equally to trigger off its productive mechanisms.

Certainly a great deal must be conceded, if the different types of current architecture are any guide. Whenever it finds itself in conflict with systems of building construction or the interests of landed property or the principle of maximum profit, modern architecture too falls in with the requirements of the client who wants what is familiar, with scarcely a trace of aesthetic innovation.

Not even our supposed technological objectivity which plays such an important part in the production of current objects escapes from this vicious circle. Kitsch is at work as much in the physical exuberance of certain buildings as in the extravagant futility of various gadgets. The vast living-room in the villa where Goldfinger, in the film of the same name, planned the robbery of the gold in Fort Knox, could be completely transformed by technology. The means were completely disproportionate to the ends, but the degree of mechanical and electrical control was such that screens appeared, doors closed, trapdoors opened and lights and television came on, all at the flick of a finger. This is the true projection of that spiteful lust for power which midcult evinces and technics express: the two combine to produce an architecture built purely for effect and devoid not only of meaning but lacking even practical use. A similar outcome in both the rural and the urban contexts is the blight resulting from the private use of the automobile. There is then an enormous range of objects which are constructed on kitsch lines, but which derive originally from the pure handling of formal elements: the recollection of feeling which becomes a souvenir, the symbolic transference, which seeks initially to obtain literary testimony for an object, but which ends up as a purely visual interpretation of it, the superfluity of communication, the purely stylistic character, effete in terms of principle but fresh in terms of effect, and the use of self-contradictory technical and formal terms of reference taken out of context and reorientated towards consumer use pure and simple. These new factors comprise in general a means of communication which asserts and confirms its attachment to a particular class and to certain well-defined categories: luxury, modernity, right-thinking, good education and the sort of places which have already acquired picture postcard status.

228 The fantasy science fiction city
of the future used as an advertisement for ceiling lighting camouflages the
ridiculous futility of gadgetry by its
supposed technological objectivity.

229 The sleep of reason breeds monsters:
reason can doze off, but in some cases it is
deliberately drugged by the presumption
that it can offer an alternative to the
stylistic uniformity of mass production.
Having challenged preconceived ideas of
the 'beautiful' and justified what is ugly,
one thus tries to base the aesthetic
argument on an attempt at an
aesthetic of the freakish.
It is fortunate that the word 'kitsch'
exists. In the illustration, a walnut show-
case with Fiat 600 doors.

230 The 'custom-built' car, a luxury speed monster, is the true symbol of kitsch with its monumental elephantiasis and formal allure.

231 Reference to modern sculpture and the fact that the egg is more resilient than the sphere enabled two young architects to give vent to their feelings in this way.

The catalytic process is once again characterized in these instances by the use of an already existing framework in a context of disruptive effects, but instead of forming a collage based on constructive and creative principles it degenerates into simple transposition; it is in this way that parts of Mondrian's pictures come to be used as posters or chair-covers and Klee's innovations produce decorative motifs for bar seats; the effect produced is one of confusion rather than of

232 Someone had the idea of decorating the grey and squalid façade of a block of flats with a Mondrian-inspired panel.

desecration. At one time for example aerodynamic principles were applied as a symbol of modernity to the design of such static objects as radios, electric irons and hair-driers. A great part of present-day styling, (over and above such purpose as the process serves as a means of mass communication), resolves itself into an operation geared purely to the stimulation of consumption.

Until such time as production processes and the designers themselves take into account the publicity aspect of the industrial design as well as the planning factors, the object will remain an ornament or a piece of window-dressing, or will only project in a fanfare of chrome and flashing lights the image of a status symbol destined by a swift process of obsolescence to become a typical example of kitsch.

But whether in the case of paintings or sculpture critical attention

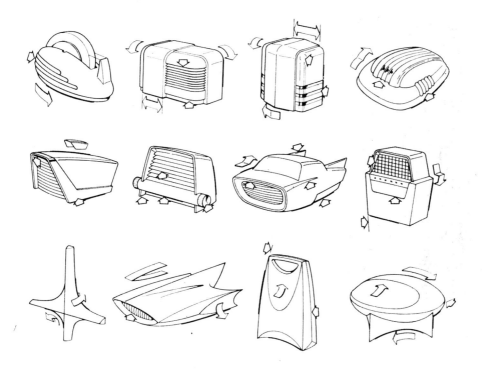

233 Much of the styling of a consumer object is simply sales promotion.

is focused on the differing formative influences of a kitsch object or an artistic object, equal importance must nevertheless be attributed, particularly from the design aspect, to the purpose for which the object is intended, the attitudes which it induces and the relationship between these attitudes and the meaning which the object acquires through use. In fact, whether the presence or otherwise of

267

an awareness of kitsch in a viewer or a reader leaves the painting or the book unaffected and available to others, in the case of architecture it makes, on the contrary, a direct intervention as a disruptive influence. To the extent that in architecture use and meaning, treatment and sense, object and attitude are two sides of the same coin, kitsch-man has a profound bearing on the definition of the meaning of architecture and design, either in its treatment or as a direct influence.

What then can be done for instance to rescue a collection of splendid individual works accumulated without discrimination or scattered over a space which is by its very nature unsuitable for the crowd, from the clutches of kitsch? What can be done to fix the meaning of an object within a total context in the presence of someone who identifies it with social ambitions or worse, and stultifies its very essence?

It is already possible to refer to kitsch in this sense in relation to building types: the predilection for a particular layout or a particular arrangement of the accommodation or a special relationship between the building and its environment is already a valid force within this context.

The apartment block, the villa, the suburban family home, which still obstinately retains vestigial traces of the sense of private ownership and pride of possession, are straightforward examples of kitsch in relation to the object and the attitudes which it induces. Here, a multiplicity of decorative treatments speak with a babel of tongues, and wealth and luxury are reflected in a despairing use of literary allusion in a desperate search for personal identity, and in a set pattern of materials compressed into far too small a dimensional scale in a forlorn attempt to restore in an attenuated and purely symbolic form earlier functions and freedoms within the sphere of the dwelling. It would be interesting to trace the history of the various elements of the dwelling and their actual as well as their apparent functions; to analyze the relationship between the various parts and to establish their functions of concealment or revelation. The motivation behind them would soon be apparent and could easily be related to that kitsch attitude which aims to establish between itself and the rest of the world a justification of conventionality and its recognition on a formal basis. Faced with new conceptions of building exploitation produced by midcult, the neo-Gothic villa and the sham *fin-de-siècle* mansion maintain a dignity which benefits their theatricality, but which today hides behind the false functionalism of low-cost production. In this way, the slums of the rich pile up in continuous develop-

234 *Top left* An Egyptian style bedroom with matt lacquer on maple wood hand-painted in colour and gold; the interior is two-toned with varnished low reliefs.

235 *Top right* Even the most elegant atmosphere does not escape the sense of falsity nowadays linked with the concept of interior decoration and the personality of the designer, as in this kitsch masterpiece by one of England's leading interior decorators.

236 Given the modern concept of interior decoration, kitsch is perhaps inevitable, as in this hotch-potch in the 'modern manner'.

237 *Bottom right* The mock rustic mass-produced living-room with barrels and tubs covered with fur.

238 Compared with the new typologies invented by the midcult of building speculation, the neo-Gothic villa and the sham *fin de siècle* castle conserve a theatrical dignity of their own which is nowadays masked by mock functionalism.

ment in the suburbs or in the more central areas of the city. Structurally, they are built on the same principles as the new working-class housing which in its turn strives desperately to turn its back on its proletarian origin in an effort to regain at least the dignity of the apartment block if not the status of a private property. There is thus a dual convergence towards that mean level which forms the natural habitat of the kitsch object.

To live in a place according to kitsch rules implies a constant effort to diminish its scale and a constant search for ways to reduce the functional activities of even the great cities to domestic terms. This conception has a theoretical basis in that doctrine of townscape and street furniture which gathers in the characteristically minor elements and subsequently disgorges them refined and completely lacking both the robustness and the authenticity which they previously derived from their own form and their truly popular origins.

270

239 The 'hovels of the rich' conglomerate on the outskirts of cities.

The rules decree a code of social decorum according to which excess of any kind is expected to scandalize. Size is the governing factor in reducing things to the kitsch level. There is consequently some difficulty in assessing the significance of kitsch in architecture and design in the light of this dimensional problem. If in fact, as we have already seen, smallness of scale, fragmentation, and concentration on detail are typical requirements for the kitsch conception and enjoyment of architecture, how terrifying must seem those large-scale repetitive developments which in one fell swoop preclude all possibility of kitsch.

If a small family house on the outskirts of a large North American city, with its garden, flowers and net curtains is the very symbol of the aesthetic and sociological limits of kitsch, if the 'house beautiful' is the dream of every middle-class citizen, a hundred thousand examples of the house beautiful set cheek by jowl necessarily tran-

271

scend the private sector and reveal an extravagant and grandiose preoccupation with the question of habitation.

Kitsch is a sort of miniaturization of the front garden or park attached to the old neo-classical villa into the bourgeois citizen's little plot, but the repetition of this process reflects the repetitive features of mass-production, which in some way reduces the friction between harsh necessity and sentiment.

A pink Thunderbird, with its stylistic attributes, its monumental grossness and its explicit allure is a kitsch status symbol, but a hundred thousand cars strung along a motorway or assembled in some gigantic car-park introduce a new, if equally ugly, dimension as far as kitsch is concerned. To survive, kitsch must operate on a small individual scale. The 'souvenir as a mini-monument' referred to by Ludwig Giesz is the concentrated embodiment of richer and fuller memory contexts. Without this process of miniaturization there can be no kitsch. The restaurants strung along the highways in the United States (or in Italy, which must be the most Americanized country in the world) clearly reveal the problem of kitsch in territorial terms. The kitsch characteristics of these places do not in fact stem so much from the style of furnishing or the display of goods or their architectural treatment as from their reassuring presence in the landscape: reassuring because of the consistency of the goods which they offer and their ready comprehensibility – islands committed to the role of a home from home, which inspire confidence in the face of the unfamiliar aspect of the natural landscape by reducing it to familiar dimensions, which offer a service, restore the balance of things and minimize the adventurous element of the journey.

The perfect example of the balance between domesticity and the sense of adventure, the element of surprise and firm reassurance is the mimetic relationship between the contemporary suburban landscape and the great international fairs. The loud and colourful hubbub arises from false hopes of a better future in the fantasy world of technological progress, but the practical outcome is an offer at the exit of a coupon giving a discount on the latest superbiologicautomatic washing machine. The rustic aspect of the sham Flemish village conjures up a whole realm of fantasy, and an exotic Chinese pavilion has as its neighbour a building in the Bauhaus style. The marvellous is concentrated into a magic box of extravagant proportions which projects into the future as well as into the past the idea of exceptional discoveries and acquisitions. The resulting projection of the urban scene resembles a phrenetic stream of adjectives divorced from their nouns or presupposes the complete embodiment of fantasy by the

240–242 The kitsch features of motorway restaurants derive not so much from the taste of their decoration, the display of goods or the type of architecture as from their reassuring presence in the landscape; (above) one of the many restaurants scattered along the motorway; (below) a mock ship, housing a restaurant, a few miles from the coast.

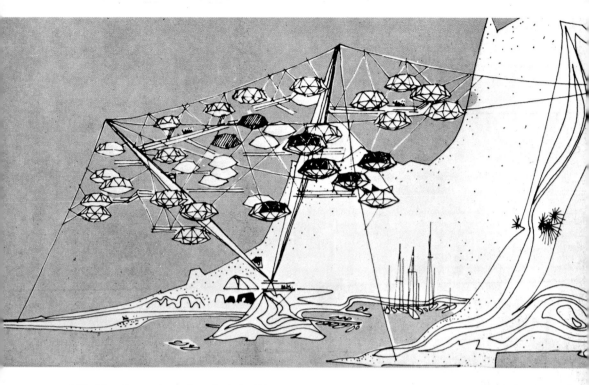

243 Kitsch utopia: a futuristic holiday resort

establishment in precise and ordered stages of an escape route into the whimsical world of Disneyland. On a smaller scale, the modern bar concentrates the various aspects of this same process: discovery, efficient service and the physical aspect of the consumption of food; china, formica, stainless steel, real and imitation wood, mirrors, glass, fabrics and marble: all decorated and all modern except perhaps for one crystal chandelier as the sole reminder of a vanishing memory; then bottles, cups, sugar and biscuits.

But generally speaking, on this dimensional scale, it is furniture which is treading the primrose path of kitsch, without hope of redemption. The most refined environment along with the most wretched caricature of modern taste does not escape that impression of the false or meretricious with which furniture is associated nowadays.

◄ 244 Huge international fairs project the balance between domesticity and futuristic discovery which often projects hopes for a better future on the imaginary plane of technological possibility.

275

Nothing is more ludicrous than that retreat which occurs with increasing frequency, from the concept of design to one of 'furnishing', or to put it even better, the concept of the 'anti-house' which is conceived from the inside and demonstrates at best a lack of cohesion between the interior and the exterior or at worst a deplorable falsity of architectural conception and a design which has been swamped by a typical kitsch operation: the furnishings have the qualities of a number of useless even if high-class adjectives, which by and large are interchangeable.

Once the feeling of social necessity is lost, the course of quality comes to depend on a consensus of approval within the framework of a social relationship, and on an argument in which the social climate precludes the possibility of dissent, and there is left behind only the echo of the inevitable stereophonic background music. Kitsch thus becomes in itself the whole essence of the operation because the project is hardly inspired with the feeling of necessity.

Nevertheless, I would not want this argument to appear as a futile accusation against poor imitations or creative sterility.

Kitsch augments the variety of forms present in the world very considerably, and at the same time substantially reduces their significance, but kitsch is not to be numbered among the things which rational thought has shown to be recoverable, if only in the form of basic materials, and adaptable for other purposes. Kitsch is, on the contrary, one of the invalid sociological and aesthetic techniques concerned with the production and enjoyment of things. These techniques are themselves based on an invalid social relationship and an inherent lack of clarity. This, as we have seen, can only be expressed by kitsch, which does not accept the nature of things in the light of their critical or revelatory attributes, but to the extent which they cover and protect, relieve and console.

TRADITIONAL KITSCH

Traditional kitsch *by Gillo Dorfles*

There is a traditional – or rather a so-called traditional – type of kitsch that has virtually become a commonplace. All the writings and publications which have been concerned with the problem of bad taste usually dwell on this type, which – though this must be said with the utmost caution – is probably less dangerous than the other more insidious forms which we have examined so far.

In this anthology – in which we cannot unfortunately accommodate another type of traditional kitsch: literary kitsch, for reasons which have already been outlined – this chapter is essential; but we have preferred to put it at the end of the book so as to show that it is relatively unimportant and in a certain sense inoffensive.

Even if 'garden gnomes' – coloured terracotta statuettes based on gnomes, elves and Disney characters – will continue to be sold (and bought) for several years or decades, there is no doubt that before long even the people who buy them today will realize that they are no longer 'in' if they do, so will avoid committing such a vulgar error as that of decorating their gardens with gnomes or their drawing rooms with alabaster models of the Leaning Tower of Pisa. Alas, other forms of kitsch will come and are already here, in fact, replacing the traditional ones: we have seen this in the pages of this book. And so we need shed no tears over the passing of traditional kitsch. On the contrary it would be quite within the bounds of possibility that within a few decades the same thing will happen to the gnomes as has happened to some – genuinely artistic – Art Nouveau objects, which, having gone unrecognized and been relegated to attics, are now being revalued and put on the market at very high prices in auctions and by antique dealers.

Recovery will be harder for the deprived garden gnomes produced in hundreds and thousands by some craftsman's oven: it would need a cataclysm to annihilate most of them, leaving just a few as a testimony of a highly kitsch age such as ours.

Aleksa Čelebonović has been involved with the problem of kitsch at various times, which is why we thought of him for this concluding chapter. He is a director of a large publishing house in Belgrade and an art critic, and has published many essays on the theory of modern art, a volume on contemporary Yugoslavian painting and an essay called *Towards the Arts*. In addition he has made a series of television films on ancient art.

◀ 245 A traditional kitsch factory

Notes on traditional kitsch

by Aleksa Čelebonović

From the moment when man invented machines for the industrial reproduction of various types of objects, a gap was formed between man's sensitivity to material and his actual moulding of it. The conflict of form and structure, as the phenomenon is defined by P. Francastel, has manifested itself most disconcertingly of all in the area where sentiment plays a primary role: in objects ostensibly created so as to offer aesthetic enjoyment. Included in this group, apart from paintings and statuettes, are objects which have no real use or meaning; in short, the whole conglomeration of knick-knacks which offers the guest of a comfortable family an image of well-being and allows the masters of the house to abandon themselves to a game imbued with a puerile and immature imagination. It is interesting to note that the production of all these objects, souvenirs, animals, sickly statuettes, non-functional tumblers and dinner services, originating as it does from the nineteenth century, still continues today in spite of everything – and it is not a great deal – that has been done in the field of industrial design.

The development of techniques, with all the ensuing results, has made it possible at relatively modest expense for any sort of idea that crosses the minds of uncultured people to be realized. There is nothing that cannot feasibly be manufactured in one way or another, which is why a situation has been created in which the interests of the manufacturer coincide with those of a great mass of people who have no affinity with the genuine values of the past, the study of history and the principles inherent in the use of materials. Neither party pays any attention to the relationship between form and matter, nor, even worse, are they interested in genuinely expressive and functional forms, for the simple reason that they are incapable of understanding them. Instead of authentic pieces they are content with modified substitutes which are accordingly thought of as more beautiful: the vacuum is filled by semblance and false showiness. Like lorry drivers who decorate their cabs with cuttings from magazines to create a fictitiously beautiful world in which they can sleep in parking-places. A remarkable number of people – many more than one might suppose if one takes into account the fact that education has become compulsory in most parts of the world, and the mass of information provided by educational programmes about the progress of society – are still incapable of making the most elementary distinction between appearance and reality, between imitation and the object imitated. The features peculiar to primitive peoples and children are evident in the advanced environment of our technological civilization, thanks to the removal of those obstacles which previously hindered craftsmanship because of the unmanageable nature of the materials available; the enjoyment of kitsch objects is a secondary reflection of this phenomenon. By this we do not mean that kitsch is tied up exclusively with primitive peoples and children. On the contrary, it is precisely these groups who spontaneously create the most expressive, most authentic and most forceful type of objects, in which the link between structure and form is clearly expressed; it is also true that since they are unaware of the validity of their artistic products and are quite incapable of distinguishing between the imitation and the object imitated, these people are more easily prey to the

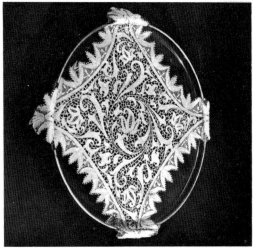

246–247 The beer-mug-cum-tower and the tray with the pseudo-lace design are two examples of a type of kitsch which has remained unchanged for more than half a century.

248–249 A ceramic negro idol and a false book become liqueur bottles complete with sets of glasses.

250 Animals lend themselves to traditional kitsch, as in these two admirable examples.

kitsch tendency, with all its baggage of lies, pretence, imitation and affectation.

I would not say that kitsch springs from any inner need in man. No, it imposes itself upon him. Kitsch has found it easy to impose itself on the uneducated and ingenuous who have not yet chosen their cultural requirements and have only made superficial attempts to find out about the possibility of satisfying them, and who have still less

282

251 *Top left* In a sculptor friend's studio, Gabriele d'Annunzio tickles this stag with obvious delight.

252–253 A cat tea-pot and a dovecote with plaster doves.

acquired fixed tastes; kitsch thus infiltrates into the mind like an infection in an organism that is incapable of resisting it. Modern economics would define this phenomenon in terms of the creation of new consumer demands due to the pressure of the market. In other words, producers of kitsch merchandise put them on sale, thereby reaching the completely unsuspecting purchaser. This is where we must ask ourselves where the reason for its success lies.

Lack of resistance and education is not enough to explain the success of kitsch. Although the immaturity of the individuals who consume it is the essential pre-condition of the whole kitsch phenomenon, immaturity is not in itself enough to define the substance of

254–255 Traditional kitsch is the same the world over: an American shop with a Pietà and dolls and a Japanese curio with pagoda and deer.

the problem with any degree of precision. If on the one hand we consider the conditions of life – we will also include here the enjoyment of cultural goods – and on the other the individual who lives in such conditions, we can state that the great majority of people avail themselves of the technical expedients of our time in good measure, especially in the fields of transport, hygiene and mass communication, while only an extremely small minority takes advantage of the progress in culture and art in this and earlier ages.

"A Chess Set of such intricacy and size would once have been hand-carved and too expensive for any but a wealthy collector"

MOST BEAUTIFUL CHESS SET WE HAVE EVER SEEN

You can judge the beauty of these sets by the pieces shown here. No wonder they have become the most *wanted* chess sets in America. Now we offer them in a wider choice of prices and sizes. From as low as $5.95!

Meticulously fashioned after the classic sculpture of Rome. The King is Augustus; the Queen, Livia; the Bishop, Cicero; the Knight, a mounted Roman Soldier; the Rook, a Forum column; the Pawn, a Roman foot soldier. They are made of styrene. Those illustrated above are silver and gold. All other sets are in Alabaster White and Granite Gray. All with felted base.

DELUXE SET: King, 4⅞" high; Queen, 4⅛"; Bishop, Knight and Rook, App. 4¼"; Pawn, 3⅜". Heavily weighted and felted. Included are folding playing board, 16⅝" square and Chess Booklet. In leatherette case, with 2 lift-out trays. .... **$14.95** *plus $1 PP & Indig.*

SPECIAL GOLD & SILVER SET: Same size as DeLuxe Set—with pieces of Antique Gold and Silver as illustrated. All pieces extra-heavily weighted and felted. Included are black-and-gold 16⅝" board & Chess Booklet. In elegant green Morocco leatherette presentation case. .... **$29.95** *plus $1 PP & Indig.*

256 A chess-set representing figures from ancient Rome gives the kitsch-man the joy of rediscovering 'historical culture' as he plays.

A certain inaccessibility which is inherent in artistic creations may also contribute to this. The art of the past is less comprehensible today than it used to be because its interpretations somehow lack contemporary significance. In paintings which were once imbued with religious significance and represented a fixed conception of the world, the uninformed spectator of today usually sees merely colours and forms, as if he were looking at – according to the well-known phrase formulated by Maurice Denis – 'a divided surface painted in

285

a certain manner'. Observations referring to this way of looking at things and, in general, to the possibility of accepting the art of the past as expressed by Jean Dubuffet are quite fundamental. In his Asphyxiante culture he shows what he has observed in the past twenty years; the art of the past, and especially that of the present, is not only inaccessible but also very boring. It becomes an object that is only venerated by an élite; suitable state-run departments are created to impose the viewpoints of this élite on the masses, who, needless to say, refute it or, a second time round, accept the results without, however, participating with any real understanding or affinity; a new and fertile field is thus opened up for kitsch. We should add at this juncture that Dubuffet's condemnation of cultural and artistic tradition is accompanied by a desire to refute the constant imitation and falsification of past products and is not, of course, meant as a glorification of traditional kitsch. By postulating that the work of art is interesting he is in fact defending the cause of imagination and championing the distinction of its products when created by the individual, he is not, of course, upholding the uniformity imposed on them by mass-production. If a knowledge of the past and a close study of it – an understanding of what has been transmitted to us – represent one of the ways of defending the individual from kitsch, the fact remains that this role can be played out solely within the framework of a cultural élite, while the 'others' are automatically condemned to become the victims of kitsch production.

This does not mean that 'the others' cannot feel inspired to imitate the élite. Ordinary people have tended, after a certain period, to accept what was previously the perogative of the aristocracy or the élite. It is common knowledge that popular dress is modelled on the costumes of the rich. The same phenomenon can be detected in interior decoration. The bourgeois family's glass-fronted dresser sparking with china and silver, glass and ivories has become the ideal of all the social strata who are not in a position to display real Dresden china, Russian silver, Murano glass and Japanese ivories. Plastic knick-knacks, plaster Buddhas, bare-breasted enamelled negresses, celluloid trays with lace engravings, successfully and much more cheaply replace objects which are in themselves quite authentic, but have been accumulated without discernment and therefore represent the first phase of kitsch. The second phase of kitsch, which I would call kitsch squared, is so obvious that we are

257–265 Unbridled kitsch publicity, taken from homes-and-gardens magazines ▶

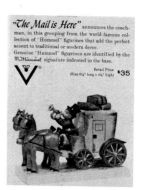

genuinely amazed that we can have been enthusiastic and eager to purchase it. We need only walk through the streets of Venice and pass by the useless kiosks offering plastic or metal San Marco campaniles and gondolas of all sizes lit by electric lanterns; or walk round the squares of any European metropolis to find an infinite number of so-called souvenirs in the most vulgar taste and evidently cheaply made. That is why the peasant's house, once faithful to the tradition of rough ceramics and copper and sturdy household furniture, has become a collection of trash from all over the world, with new furniture which is no longer cheap and an electric kitchen. There is no longer any need to travel to distant villages; we only have to think of the department store (for example) which offers Japanese, Italian, Canadian or Bulgarian goods which were once only to be had on the spot. Add to this the hoste of 'cute' objects stripped of any local or national connotations, available to everyone because of their ostensible 'universality'. Look at all the cows and dogs which are there by virtue of the loyalty and meekness of their species, as symbols of fortune and wealth; at the plastic Mickey Mice and Donald Ducks who also have a place of honour together with the china that

266 Violinists, Venuses, saints, Pinocchios and Mickey Mice ready for the huge kitsch market

is kept for special occasions; at the huge cushions of fake velvet and the hangings that majestically adorn the ample marriage bed.

Among the features peculiar to primitive man which were observed by C. G. Jung, two are also characteristic of the sort of people who enjoy the traditional kitsch object. On the one hand, primitive man projects his inner self outwards into the external world; on the other hand he is incapable of developing his awareness and of subordinating his own behaviour; in fact he is reduced to spending his time in a sort of lethargy in which his unconcious prevails, as it were. We can also see the same phenomenon in many individuals who live in a civilized society (we only have to think of the widespread circulation of traditional kitsch objects). Here too, collectors and consumers project their own inner world into the outer world. Given that their psyche is not tortured by the problems posed by life in the raw (the struggle against darkness, cold or wild beasts) their inner being is tormented by the problems of the environment in which they live: how to earn money; how to satisfy their sexual needs; how to gain prestige. Together with bad films, popular magazines etc., kitsch objects serve as a cue to project the misery of their inner world into the outer world. In this way, latent problems are projected into objects whose value is purely fictitious, because it makes things easier. They are incapable of taking in the world in which they live, and of developing their own individuality; they are not equipped to understand the language and logic of shapes; such people opt only too easily for the false splendour of vulgarity because it recalls something which lies deep down in the darkness of their desires. This choice puts them on the same level as the happiest of aborigines bartering gold and ivory for the glass beads of European traders.

267 Bismarck as a beer-mug

CONCLUSION

by Gillo Dorfles

Having reached the end (but is there an end to kitsch?) of our antho-
logical review, I should like to sum up all that has been examined in
these pages, and at the same time dedicate this last chapter to a
problem with which we have so far only sparred; the problem of the
conscious and intentional use of kitsch elements by certain contemporary artists.

In this way, one might possibly create a bridge that could unite the
two aspects of art and kitsch which are doomed, it seems, to remain
inevitably separate.

I think at least one point has emerged from the many documents
presented here and from the many articles collected together in this
volume: namely the fact that the very concept 'bad taste' refers
specifically to our age, and was not present in the past – at least in its
actual form: this, therefore, would be the main aspect of any analysis
of a kitsch phenomenology; once having recognized in it a sort of
deviation, a sort of degeneration from what – like it or not – we
should be able to consider as the 'norm' of man's ethical and aesthetic
attitude. If there is some justifiable doubt about the legitimacy of
appealing to a moral 'norm', one cannot say the same about the
existence of a standard of taste – its existence being agreed and un-
disputed in the various centuries and styles. Nowadays, though, this
standard is being increasingly violated and upset, for only in our
time has a phenomenon such as we intend to examine occurred: that
is to say the *intentional and conscious use* by top flight artists (one
can at once list important names: Duchamp, Picasso, De Chirico and
so on) of avowedly kitsch elements; not (and this is a less relevant
phenomenon but one which still troubles us) the use by a culturally
sophisticated public, of elements which are decidedly kitsch (furniture, furnishings and pictures of course, statues etc.) but which are
redeemed by the particular attitude that likes to be called 'camp',
itself, in a certain way, a rival to kitsch.

What in fact does one understand by camp? Using some of Susan
Sontag's remarks (in her 'Notes on Camp' in *Towards Interpretations
and other Essays,* Farrar, Strauss and Giroux, New York, 1966) we

◄ 268 Posters of Bobby Kennedy and reproductions of Aubrey Beardsley in a typical
camp 'landscape'

can say that: 'the essence of camp is its love of what is unnatural, artificial and excessive,' and among the works that come under this sort of 'taste' one can mention: 'the drawings of Beardsley, the works of Bellini, some of Visconti's productions, certain *fin de siècle* post-cards, Gordon's old comic strips, Guimard's entrances for the Paris Metro . . .' and, lastly, that: 'Many examples of camp from a "serious" viewpoint are bad art or kitsch. Not all, however. Not only is camp not necessarily bad art; there are also works of art which can be con-sidered camp . . . and even deserve the most serious admiration.'

Camp is therefore a special attitude, sophisticated and somewhat snobbish, which salvages material otherwise doomed (often if not always) to oblivion, or which re-evaluates what, *per se,* would only have had scant artistic value and cultural interest.

Camp, at all events, is a phenomenon that is merely of passing interest to us here: we can consider it only in its manifestation as anti-kitsch, given that in the last analysis one could not even conjecture about the existence of a camp attitude if there were no possibility of salvaging kitsch, or, in general, neglected and deviating artistic elements.

I hope it will be clear from what has already been said about kitsch in the home, in nature, in tourism etc. that both camp and kitsch can be considered as direct offspring of the consumer society in which we live. The affluent society which, with all its gaps and faults, is in a position to give each one of us (and of course we must hope that this will be so not only in the industrialized West, but also in the 'third' and even in a 'fourth' world!) a refrigerator and a wireless, TV and a car, is at the same time responsible for many of the crimes of our times: the brazen styling of the bodywork of cars, the vulgarity of tourism, the inhuman horror of summer beaches and winter ski-ing resorts, and, similarly, the newly-weds' bedroom furniture, American kitchens, hordes of garden gnomes and rabbits and Disneyland characters, the Swiss-miniature phenomenon and so on. To what, if not to the affluent society, are all these things due?

But – and in these concluding pages we pose ourselves the question once again – should we then look forward to a return to the pre-industrial era, to a condition which we can find in certain backward regions which are still untouched by our deplored and deplorable 'civilization of well-being'?

Certainly not: there is, everywhere, a kitsch of lack of elegance, of cultural retrogression and of industrial and artistic non-up-to-dateness which is often equivalent to out-and-out bad taste. And so the present revolt – certainly legitimate – against consumer society, against the manipulation of mass taste from the top, against designers' subservience to industry, is being carried on in an attempt to end the struggle to restore man's cultural autonomy on all levels, to salvage the creative as well as the fruitful qualities which the individual should be able to display at will, to liberate art from the schemes imposed by industrialization, commercialism and monopolistic economy, be it private or state-owned.

The moment for redeeming kitsch is thus some way off and will only come about – I should like to hope this even if there is nothing to guarantee it – when we have got the better both of the dire poverty and the lack of food that are afflicting much of the third world today (and not only the third world), and of the opulent wealth of 'advanced' industrial society (as we like to call it, without thinking that this society is anything but advanced, except in its widespread conformism) that is afflicting the rest of mankind. The reintroduction of an age in which art comes to have not only a commercial (or snobbish) effect and in which imitation is no longer a necessity imposed by the market is still a long way off; let us hope that we shall soon detect the first warning signs.

But let us now consider the last case for which kitsch is, indirectly, responsible: when it is used *intentionally and consciously* by the very artists or people of today who, precisely because of their awareness of the existence of kitsch, make use of it for diametrically opposed ends.

The attempt by some artists to redeem kitsch, intentionally and consciously, in their work is worthy but two-edged; in fact if this sort of operation acquires the all the more tasty flavour of 'forbidden fruit' for those who belong to the cultural élite, the same operation can lead to two different misunderstandings for those who are not so well-informed:

1) the belief that the object made by such artists via their method of using subject matter out of context, is authentically in 'good taste' (for example if Rauschenberg or Jasper Johns use a bottle of Coca Cola in one of their works the belief that this is, *per se,* an artistic object);

2) the even more dramatic confusion of art and non-art (for example, if Baj uses stage backcloths painted by some hack at so much per yard as the background for some of his works, it must be appreciated that one should praise even such landscapes with their *clair-de-lune* or Bay-of-Naples-with-Vesuvius theme done by a romantic painter to old naturalistic designs). These two examples make it clear what type of art I am going to refer to: to all those creative forms which first

293

appeared around the beginning of the century and were introduced by the 'great' exponents of the various European 'isms'. I am thinking, for example, of some of Balla's famous pieces of furniture which were recently re-appraised and which are, stylistically speaking, of great interest, but have an undeniable kitsch note; or of some of Duchamp's *objets trouvés*, coat-stands and urinals for example, the 'demystifying' value of which was very considerable but which, taken for what they really were (and not for what they 'became' through the process of detaching them from their environment and revaluation by the artist), are no more than banal objects in the worst taste. I am also thinking of a whole series of objects used by the first wave of

269 *Lunch in fur* by Meret Oppenheim (1938)

Surrealists (like Meret Oppenheim's famous fur table-service – plate 269) and just as much of some of the famous and apparently naturalistic compositions by Magritte (plate 270), Delvaux, Labisse etc. . . . which, with their blatant anti-naturalistic and anti-conformist purpose, nourished the emergence of a camp attitude towards works and objects which belong strictly to the best of kitsch.

And if one refers to more recent manifestations, how can one deny

294

270 *Quand l'heure sonnera*
(When the hour strikes) by
René Magritte

the presence of kitsch elements in many of the works of major American pop artists? Some of Oldenburg's gigantic 'soft' still-lifes; some of Rauschenberg's stuffed eagles; some of Wesselmann's lowest-grade advertizing posters with their nudes; Kienholz's bar and other of his environments (which by themselves are enough to give us a condensed idea of USA kitsch atmosphere); and some of Lichtenstein's recent poster imitations (the first examples of which, made from blowing-up

295

271 In Warhol's Mona Lisas the kitsch-myth is re-presented in the Pop manner, as in the Jackies (plate 272).

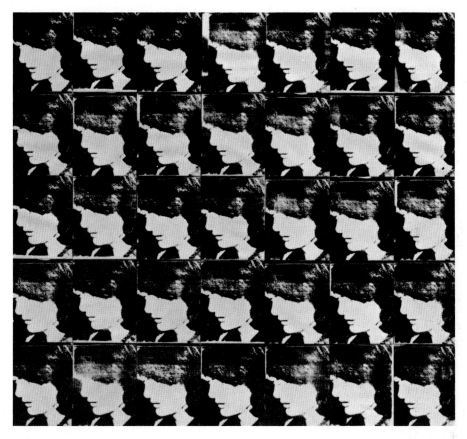

272 Andy Warhol's portrait of Jackie (1965). Leo Castelli Collection, New York

his famous comic-strips, were never kitsch anyway, the languid sunsets of his *Landscapes* (plates 273-4); and lastly, Warhol's *Mona
Lisas,* with the myth presented in a pop manner (the pictures repeated
on the canvas almost geometrically) as with the Marilyn Monroes
and the Jackie Kennedys, almost as if the three personalities were
linked by a common history (plates 271-2). The pop process which
has been of decisive importance in the recent artistic scene has, in
fact, brought to light two apparently contradictory facts:

297

1) the way in which modern man – especially in the USA – is surrounded almost everywhere by kitsch elements which he does not even notice (the European arriving for the first time in the USA notices them before the grandiose character of the general prospect and the robustness of certain new perspectives have completely annulled his own 'historical' sensitivity which, on the first approach, was jolted by this massive presence of kitsch);

2) the way in which, on the other hand, these same kitsch elements have an undeniable charm of their own which – where they have been used out of context – is translated into the authentic work of art.

273–274 An awarenesss of kitsch is often present in the work of Roy Lichtenstein, *(left) Night Seascape*, 1966; *(right) My Reverie*, 1966.

275 The intentional and quite conscious salvage of pictorial kitsch material used ▶ as a collage is one of the stylistic features of Baj's painting.

Think, for example, of the plastic-chromatic (and therefore aesthetic) value of juke-boxes, automatic pin-tables, luminous signs, all those domestic gadgets which are the basis of a whole ABC of pre-established 'signs', which have been widely used by the various American pop artists and later by their European imitators (Raysse, Spoerri, Fahlstrom, Arman, etc.).

A similar process, which happened some time before the flowering of Pop Art in America, is that successful attempt by Enrico Baj in his various series: *Generals, Ladies, Ultra-bodies, Furniture*. Even if Baj started from a conception that differed considerably from that of the pop artists, he, too, was frequently concerned with the use of collage material which, initially, generally had kitsch characteristics (various flower-patterned mattress materials, wall-paper and ordinary or valuable carpets; the use, already mentioned, of oil-painted backcloths (plate 275); or, again, using decorations, medals and festoons which belonged to the days of our grandfathers, but rejecting the most dissonant and vulgar aspects). The intentional and quite conscious re-introduction of this out-of-date material, which is often in 'bad taste', has enabled this Milanese artist to create his own very personal style, which often achieves an extremely refined harmony of composition, precisely because of the unusual use of such elements.

Examples of the work of some of the best of contemporary American and European pop artists, like Baj and one or two others (I can think of some of Del Pezzo's early works; some of Gaul's collages, some of Peter Blake's and Richard Hamilton's compositions which use ordinary prints or pictures borrowed from comics), contain the often insidious and subtly dangerous presence of the kitsch element. It being my intention to illustrate this element in this final chapter, I think this needs stressing. And I hope it is once again quite clear that my intention is also to point out the *positive* aspects of the presence of kitsch elements and not just the countless examples of negative aspects: i.e. those in which even well-known and generally respected contemporary artists *unintentionally* and completely unconsciously create work in undeniable 'bad taste', work which is bought at high prices by collectors, welcomed by museums and to which justice will only be done by posterity. I said at the very beginning of this volume that I did not intend to deal with work in bad taste created by contemporary artists, because it will be up to posterity and not up to us to pass a final and more reliable judgement on them; but it should not surprise anyone that the art of our time can, and indeed should, be cursed by the vampire kitsch; all of us alive today are or can be its prey, most of all the person who

300

vom
Kitsch

zur
Funktion

ALUMINIUM

276 A unique case of the conscious
use of kitsch in advertising

believes he is creating works of art when he is in fact creating mere kitsch objects.

With these last remarks about the unique phenomenon – which is at least partly positive – of kitsch in the work of art of today, I shall bring this review to a close.

How far have I succeeded in illuminating what is certainly one of the crucial problems in the history of art and aesthetics today? Unfortunately, even if some light has been shed, this will certainly not penetrate to the vast, boundless legion of kitsch-men who create and enjoy what should be the works of art of our time in a mistaken way all over the world. How then is one to open mankind's eyes to lapses and inadequacies when both are an integral part of its existence in the world, of its very way of seeing the world? Perhaps the kitsch attitude – both in its objective realizations and in its subjective aspects – belongs 'by right' to our age; and perhaps that communicative and expressive phenomenon that we insist on defining as 'art' (that so overwhelmingly dominated the ages preceding our own), is destined to adopt the kitsch aspect more than any other in the present phase of western civilization. Which does not mean that one should despair for the future of art nor that one should not support it and look forward to its recovery.

We shall be satisfied if these pages and illustrations are read and appreciated by those who are already outside kitsch and aware of its existence. And let us hope on the contrary that with the evolution and progress of present-day society, with the maturating of a new attitude towards art and the relationship between art and society and art and nature, we shall, in the not too distant future, rediscover that balance between technology and art, between art and life, which in other ages established a contemporary constant.

302

Bibliography

The bibliography of kitsch is as yet relatively small, although in recent years the number of articles and essays on the subject has increased dramatically. Among the basic works on kitsch we must cite above all Hermann Broch's *'Einige Bemerkungen zum Problem des Kitsches'* (reproduced in this volume as 'Notes on the problem of kitsch'), from *Dichten und Erkennen,* Vol. 1, Rhein-Verlag, Zurich, 1955, and Ludwig Giesz's *Phänomenologie des Kitsches. Ein Beitrag zur anthropologischen Aesthetik,* Rothe Verl. Heidelberg 1960, which from the philosophical angle constitutes a major contribution to the subject. Besides these we should mention Walther Killy's essay *Deutscher Kitsch,* Vandenhoeck and Ruprecht, Göttingen 1961.

The following works should also be noted:
Gustav E. Pazaurek, *Guter und schlechter Geschmack im Kunstgewerbe,* Stuttgart, 1912
F. Karpfen, *Der Kitsch, Eine Studie über die Entartung der Kunst,* Hamburg, 1925
Hans Reimann, *Das Buch vom Kitsch,* Monaco, 1936
J. Reisner, *Ueber den Begriff Kitsch* (thesis for the University of Göttingen), 1955
Gillo Dorfles, *Le Oscillazioni del gusto,* Milan, 1958
Karl Markus Michel, *'Gefühl als Ware, Zur Phänomenologie des Kitsches',* in *Neue Deutsche Hefte,* 57, 1959
Harold Rosenberg, 'Pop culture: a review of Kitsch' in *The Tradition of the New,* Horizon Press, New York, 1959; Thames and Hudson, London, 1962.
Clement Greenberg, 'Avant garde and kitsch' in *Art and Culture,* Beacon Press, Boston, 1961 (An extract from this is in this anthology)
Edgar Morin, *L'esprit du temps,* Paris, 1962.
Gillo Dorfles, *'Kitsch e cultura'* in *Aut Aut,* 1, 1963
Gillo Dorfles, *'Per una fenomenologia del cattivo gusto'* in *Rivista di Estetica,* IX.3, 1964
Umberto Eco, *'I parenti poveri'* in *Il Diario minimo,* Milan 1964
Hans E. Holthusen, *'Ueber den sauren kitsch'* now in *Der Unbehauste Mensch,* 1964

Umberto Eco, *'La struttura del cattivo gusto'* in *Apocalittici e Integrati,* 1965

Gillo Dorfles, *Nuovi Riti, Nuovi Miti,* chap. III. Turin, 1965

Daniel J. Boorstin, *The Image: Or What Happened to the American Dream,* Atheneum, New York, 1962; Penguin, Harmondsworth, 1965

Galvano della Volpe, *La Critica del gusto,* Milan, 1963 (1966)

The review *Magnum* (DuMont Schauberg, Cologne) produced a special number devoted to kitsch in August 1961. The information bulletin of the Biblioteca Civica di Cusano Milanino published an essay on kitsch with illustrations, signed by Ferruccio Maraspin, in No. 4 of April 1967. In 1966 a 33rpm record entitled *Mit Kitsch leben* was produced by Calig Verlag in Monaco.

List of illustrations

306

Index

Other works by Gillo Dorfles

Discorso tecnico delle arti, Nistri-Lischi, Pisa 1951
Barocco nell'architettura moderna, Tamburini, Milan 1952
Bosch, Mondadori, Milan 1953
L'architettura moderna, Garzanti, Milan 1954 (1962⁴)
Dürer, Mondadori, Milan 1958
Constantes técnicas de las artes, Nueva Vision, Buenos Aires 1958
Le oscillazioni del gusto, Lerici, Milan 1958 (1967)
Il divenire delle arti, Einaudi, Turin 1959 (1967³)
Ultime tendenze dell'arte d'oggi, Feltrinelli, Milan 1961
Simbolo comunicazione consumo, Einaudi, Turin 1962 (1967²)
Il disegno industriale e la sua estetica, Cappelli, Bologna 1963
Nuovi riti, nuovi miti, Einaudi, Turin 1965
L'estetica del mito, Mursia, Milan 1967
Artificio e natura, Einaudi, Turin 1968